In the Name of Allah,
the Compassionate, the Merciful,
Praise be to Allah, Lord of the Universe,
and Peace and Prayers be upon
His Final Prophet and Messenger.

**Imam Ali
Ibn Abi Talib**

Imam Ali
Ibn Abi Talib:

The First Intellectual Muslim Thinker

Muhammad Abdul Rauf, Ph.D.

© Copyright by Muhammad Abdul-Rauf

U.S.A.
AL-SAADAWI PUBLICATIONS
P.O. Box 4059
Alexandria, VA 22303
Tel: (703) 329-6333
Fax: (703) 329-8052

LEBANON
AL-SAADAWI PUBLICATIONS
P.O. Box 135788
Sakiat Al-Janzir
Vienna Bldg., Vienna St.
Beirut, Lebanon
Tel: 860189, 807779

All rights reserved. No part of this publication may be reproduced, stored in retrieval system, or transmitted in any form or by any means, electronic, mechanical, photo-copying, recording or otherwise, without the prior permission of the publisher.

Imam Ali Ibn Abi Talib
ISBN #1-881963-49-7

First printing, 1995

Printed in the USA

Table of Contents

Foreword xi
Introduction xv

Chapter I: Childhood 1
    Arabia 1
    Makkah and the Ka`bah 2
    The Imam's Descent 2
    Ali's Birth and Upbringing 3

Chapter II: Ali as a Teenager 5
    Young Ali Embraces Islam 5
    Reaction to Public, Open Declaration of Islam 6
    Retiring for Prayers with the Prophet 6
    Persecution of the Muslims in Makkah 7
    The Prophet's Life Threatened 8
    Young Ali Sleeps in the Prophet's Place 9
    The Prophet Hides in a Cave 10
    The Prophet Cautiously Proceeds
        on the Hijrah Journey 11

**Chapter III: Ali's Emigration to Yathrib,
"Al-Madinah"** 13
    Young Ali Leads a Party to Al-Madinah 13
    Safe Arrival of Imam Ali's Party in Al-Madinah 15

Chapter IV: The Third Decade 16
    The Imam's Involvement 16
    Serving the Prophet as a Scribe 16
    United with the Prophet in a Special
        Brotherly Tie 17
    Ali's Marriage to Fatimah 18
    The Four Most Meritorious Women 18
    Proceeding of the Marriage Ceremony 19
    Children Begotten through That Blessed Marriage 22
    The Imam Undertakes Missions on Behalf
        of the Prophet 22

Chapter V: The Imam's Unmatched Valor..........25
On the Eve of the Hijrah 25
On the Way to Al-Madinah 25
On the Day of Badr 26
On the Day of Uhud 28
During the Battle of the Ditch 29
Writing down Al-Hudaibiyah Agreement 32
On the Day of the Conquest of Makkah 34
The Prophet Visits Umm Hani' 37
The Imam: A Peace Maker 38
Standing Firm at the Critically Grave Moment
on the Day of Hunain 38
The Prophet Returns to Al-Madinah 40
Tabuk Expedition 40
Presiding over the Prophet's Funeral Service 41

Chapter VI: Merits of the Imam as Conveyed in Al-Qur'an and Al-Hadith
From the Holy Qur'an 44
Prophetic Hadiths Concerning the Imam 49

Chapter VII: 11 - 35 AH (632 - 656 AD) 53
Status of the Imam during This Era, and Rise
of the Question of the Caliphate 53
Function of the Caliph 53
The Imam's High Qualifications 54
Factors Causing Delay in the Imam's Election to the
Post of the Caliphate 55
The Imam's Reaction to the Election of Abu Bakr 57
Caliph Abu Bakr Sought the Imam's Advice 58
Caliph Abu Bakr Invites the Imam to Address
the Troops Going to Syria 59
Abu Bakr's Tremendous Services 60
Abu Bakr Appoints Umar as His Successor 61
Uthman Ibn Affan: The Third Caliph 61
Uthman's Grave Trust of the Umayyads 63
Imam Ali's Restrain 63
Blessings of the Imam's Neutrality during This Era 64
The Imam Was the Founder of the Branches
of Islamic Knowledge 66

Chapter VIII: Imam Ali Ibn Abi Talib:
The Fourth Caliph 69
His Election to the Post of the Caliphate 69

The Imam's Inaugural Address 70
A Hopeful Aspiration 71
Relief of the Provincial Governors 71
Mu`awiyah Disobeys.. 71
Serious Cleavage by Three Senior Companions.................................. 74
Ummu Salamah Warns `A'ishah 74
The Imam Struggles to Clear the Misunderstanding:
   The Camel Battle (near Al-Basrah) 75
The Battle at Siffin... 78
Arbitration and Consequences 80
The Out-Goers (Al-Khawarij or the Kharijites.................................... 84
Treacherous Murder of the Great Imam! 85
An Intrigue to Slay the Three Major Political Figures 86
Mu`awiyah and `Amr Ibn al-`As Escape Death 86
Only the Imam Becomes the Victim!... 87
The Imam's Bequest... 89
Echo of the Imam's Death... 92
The Imam's Children 96
The Imam's Intense Intelligence 98
The Imam's Ability to Respond with Persuasive Answers 100
The Imam's Mathematical Brilliance... 100

Chapter IX: Selections from the Jewel-Like
Words of the Imam 103

Foreword

The heroic figure of Ali ibn Abi Talib, may peace be upon him, is etched upon the minds and hearts of Muslims, Sunni and Shi`ite alike, as at once saint and incomparable warrior, caliph and planter of palm trees, commentator upon the Blessed Qur'an and founder of religious disputation and the science of *kalam*, originator of Arabic calligraphy and the supreme embodiment of spiritual chivalry or *futuwwah*. His two-pronged sword *Dhu'l-fiqar*, symbolizing both exoteric and esoteric authority, has been famous throughout Islamic history. His very blood still flows in the bodies of the numerous descendants of the Blessed Prophet, the *sadat* or *shurafa'* who are the fruits of the union between Ali and the radiant daughter of the Prophet, Fatimah, and who are spread throughout the Islamic world. His tomb in Najaf, a major site of pilgrimage, remains to this day, and despite all the recent tragedies, a most important religious center and a university with a millenial history.

He has been celebrated through countless poems in Arabic, Persian, Turkish, Urdu and many other Islamic languages and numerous prose works have been written and continue to be composed on him in these tongues while his own *Nahj al-Balaghah* remains to this day a source of religious inspiration as well as a model of eloquence in Arabic prose which some of the most illustrious writers of Arabic have emulated over the centuries. He has been seen and continues to be viewed by the Muslim faithful exactly as the Blessed Prophet described him in the famous *hadith*: "I am the city of Knowledge and Ali is its gate."

And yet this gate to prophetic knowledge, the Lion of God (*Asadallah*) who continues to exercise such a profound influence upon the lives of countless Muslims to this day is hardly known in the West. While numerous biographical studies have been devoted in European languages to figures who are like the dust of the feet of Ali, very few works exist in these languages which bring out the religious significance of this exemplary figure and paint an outline of his spiritual character on the basis of both knowledge and piety and in such a manner that it would be recognizable by those in the Islamic world who are familiar with the religious personality of Ali and who have smelled the perfume of his spirituality.

The present work by Dr. Muhammad Rauf is therefore particularly precious in that it is one of the very few books to fill this void. The author, a noble and gentle scholar, combines complete mastery over the traditional Arabic sources concerning the life and work of Ali, as well as details of early Islamic history which sets the background for his life, with long experience in teaching Islam, its doctrines and history, to Western audiences in both America and Europe. The result of the conjunction of these qualities is a work that is scholarly and at the same time embellished with the ornament of piety. It introduces the reader not only to the facts about the life of Ali, but also unveils something of the spiritual presence and one might say barakah of this incredible figure in whom so many diverse virtues were combined and in whose being one sees the wedding of the perfection of the contemplative and active lives and the continuation of what Islamic esoterism calls the Muhammadan Light (*al-nur al-muhammadi*).

It is of some significance that the author is an Egyptian, from a land devoted to the Family of the Prohet (*ahl al-bayt*) and that he studied at al-Azhar University established by the Fatimids whose very name derives from that of Ali's wife, a university which is just a few yards away from the Mausoleum where the head of Ali's son is buried, that is, Ra's al-Husayn, the religious heart of Cairo and in fact all of Egypt. While being nearly completely Sunni and specifically Shafi`ite, the Egyptians have a love for the *ahl an-bayt* which in its own way is no less intense than that of the Persians or Iraqis who are predominantly Shi`ite. Someting of this love is also reflected in this book, making it a precious addition to the literature of Islam in English.

All students of Islam must be grateful to Dr. Rauf in writing this simple and yet informative, scholarly and at the same time religiously moving book. He has added yet another important work to his *opera* which have stretched over several decades and whose production has continued despite all the adversities which earthly life has put before his path. This is itself proof of the fact that he is a veritable Islamic scholar always reliant upon the Divine Will and active in this world to actualize that Will, aware of the transience of life while never losing sight of the Immutable and the Eternal. May God grant him a long life and the energy to continue the task of presenting authentic works on Islam in English of which the present book is the latest and one of the most important among his extensive writings.

Seyyed Hossein Nasr
Bethesda, Maryland
September 1994

Introduction

In the name of Almighty Allah, the Merciful, the Compassionate. Praise be to Him, and may peace and blessings be upon His Messenger, Prophet Muhammad, son of Abd Allah, and upon his family and Companions.

This essay is presented on the life and legacy of one of the most illustrious Companions of the Prophet: Imam Ali Ibn Abi Talib ... a man said to have been blessed with extraordinary strength and reputed to have picked up during a battle, a heavy door and used it as a shield when his own shield was shattered. And when the troops under his command needed to climb over a high wall to cross to the enemies' fort, he picked up a huge gate and let it rest on the wall for his men to climb to the fort. It is said that only forty men could move it later when the hostilities were over.

Yet, the Imam was a model of the virtues of modesty, piety, charity, and magnanimity. He declined to dwell in the governor's residence in Al-Kufah, his capital in Iraq, and preferred to stay in the open air. He could afford to enjoy the best food and to wear the finest material, but he refused to eat bread softer than that the Prophet used to eat or to wear material finer than that the poor among his subjects could afford.

Imam Ali was the most learned person among the Prophet's Companions, as certified by the Prophet himself who described him as the Gate of Knowledge. He was indeed the first Muslim thinker, and the founder of the various branches of Islamic studies, including literary criticism. He laid down the foundations of Arabic grammar, and was the first to conceive of the grammatical terms: "word," and its categories: "noun," "verb" and "particles," and he gave their definitions. He was impelled to do so when he heard people in Al-Kufah making grammatical errors in their speeches. The chains of teachers of those scholars at whose hands the various divisions of studies, including monotheistic theology, `Ilm Al-Tawhid, and jurisprudence, `Ilm Al-Fiqh, can be traced to him, often through his cousin `Abd Allah Ibn `Abbas.

Owing to his precedence in the academic field, Ali Ibn Abi Talib alone was given the title Imam, "The Leader". It is an academic as well as a religious leadership which the Imam very well deserved.

During the lifetime of the Prophet, peace and blessings be upon him, Imam Ali, as we shall see, figured out prominently at all fronts, making a crucial contribution to Islam's survival and success. Yet, mainly due to his relatively young age, the Imam was not elected to the post of the Caliphate soon after the Prophet's death in spite of his great virtues and excellent qualities. So, Abu Bakr, then sixty-one years old, was made the First Caliph, followed by Umar Ibn Al-Khattab. When Umar was murdered by an unbeliever, the Imam was approaching the age of fifty. Yet, he missed the post by sheer circumstances. And when he was after all elected at the age of fifty-eight to that lofty post by the Muslim leadership in Al-Madinah Al-Munawwarah, as was the case of his predecessors, and the Muslim world then looked forward to an era of great leaps in progress and achievements under his wise leadership, the Imam was denied the opportunity of making such achievements by severe challenges that diverted his attention and occupied his time in attempting to quell uprisings and put down unfair armed opposition until he met with violent death almost at the end of the fifth year of his reign.

In spite of those distressing challenges, the Imam remained true to his virtues. He never lost faith in Allah, and he continued to be a model of the virtues of courage, perseverance, genuine leadership, remembrance of Allah, indifference to material attractions, justice, forgiveness and magnanimity.

In the story of the great Imam and in his noble response to gruesome experiences, we, Muslims, have a greatly-inspiring model to emulate in our response to the challenges of the modern life.

None of the sources used in preparing this work gives a full account of the life of our great Imam, the details of which are scattered among those sources. Here an attempt has been made to bring those details together within two covers. However, the amount of words quoted here from those attributed to the Imam are only a drop from an ocean. Otherwise, a selection made from the Imam's speeches and sermons by a fourth century leading scholar, Al-Sharif Al-Radiyy, fills a large volume which he called, *Nahj Al-Balaghah*, "The Path to Eloquence."

We humbly bow in gratitude to Almighty Allah for His help and guidance, and pray for His forgiveness of our shortcomings.

Chapter I
Childhood

Arabia:

Let's now go back to the year 600 After Christ and take a flight to the heights rising from the shores of the Red Sea opposite of the Sudan, a region covered with mounds of shifting sands—away from the hustle and bustle of Washington and other modern cities—the western coastal part of modern Saudi Arabia.

There we shall see a wide expanse dotted with widely separated camps of a shifting mode of life, each camp made up of a few tents woven from camel hair, inhabited by small inter-related families, with their herds of camels and sheep close-by. These people could but lead a modest life dependent on camel milk and meat for food and drink, and on its skin and hair for housing and clothes. Water was non-existent except in a few oases where wells could be dug and settled human life could flourish.

Makkah and the Ka`bah:

One such settlement was particularly honored in memory of Ibrahim, "Abraham," the Prophet-Patriarch, and his son, Isma`il, "Ishmael" who together erected a memorable sacred shrine, a cubic-shaped edifice called *The Ka`bah*, "The House of Allah, (God)." The inhabitants of the entire peninsula, called the Arabs, flocked towards that shrine annually for religious and commercial activities. Moreover, Isma`il's mother, Hagar, discovered a well nearby which has been called, *Zamzam*. Availability of water from that well made life easier, and a town around it called Makkah developed over the years.

Unlike the shifting life in the Bedouin camps, life in Makkah was stable. The town derived its prestige not only from its status as the seat of the Ka`bah and Zamzam but it was also a convenient halting site for traders midway between Yemen in the South and Syria in the North, bringing along with them Indian and Chinese goods like textiles, and Syrian products like grains. The over-land trade, between these resourceful regions was important in view of the dangerous waves of the Red Sea which made it then not safely navigatable.

The Imam's Descent:

Naturally the family who became the custodians of Allah's House and served those who came along there for pilgrimage became distinguished and honored, not only in Makkah but all over Arabia. A notable figure of that family was Abd Al-Muttalib Ibn (son of) Hashim, who died in old age about the year 578 AD. He was survived, along with others, by a son called Abu Talib, and a grand-son, Muhammad, whose father Abd Allah, had died young.

Abu Talib who inherited his ancestors' noble virtues of generosity, courage and honor, and who assumed the responsibility of Muhammad's guardianship after Abd Al-Muttalib's death, married his cousin, Fatimah Binti Asad Ibn Hashim, the great grandfather of Muhammad. She conceived from him while they were in the area of Al-Haram, the only case of conception that occurred in the Sacred Sanctuary! Fatima related that ever since she conceived of that baby, she could not bend or prostrate before the idols when she went to worship them. She said that whenever she attempted to do so she felt as if the baby stretched himself inside her stomach and made her unable to bend!

If we may diverge here a little, we may add that this good lady was close to the heart of the Prophet Muhammad, peace and blessings be upon him! Not only did she embrace Islam early in Makkah but also, like her husband, Abu Talib, she lent full support to the Prophet at the time of his lonely struggle against the polytheists in Makkah. And when the Prophet emigrated to Al-Madinah, (her husband had died about two years earlier), she followed him. When she passed away later in Al-Madinah, the Prophet who treated her like a mother, gave away one of his garments and instructed that she be shrouded in it. When her grave was dug on his order, he himself descended into it, and dug out with his own hands her *lahd,* the area by the side of the grave in which the body was laid to rest. He then lay down himself in that *lahd* and prayed:

> "O Allah! Forgive my mother, Fatimah Binti Asad. Inspire her with the monotheistic word, The *Shahadah,* and open widely her entrance to Paradise!"

When the Prophet, peace and blessings be upon him was later asked why he so did, he replied:

> "I dressed her with my garment hoping she will be clothed with a dress from Paradise; and I reclined in her grave hoping that the grave pressure on her will be lightened. She cooperated with Abu Talib in supporting and in defending me."

The baby who stretched himself out in its mother's stomach was the fetus of the Imam, Ali, whose biography is the theme of this essay. So the Imam never prostrated before an idol even when he was still in his mother's stomach, more than a decade before the monotheist message was revealed to the Prophet, peace and blessing be upon him.

Ali's Birth and Upbringing:

Ali was born in Rajab, 13, BH. When he became about five years old, Muhammad, who was then about thirty, had a discussion with Al-`Abbas, another uncle of the Prophet who was fairly well to do, and discussed the economic plight of Abu Talib with him. To alleviate Abu Talib's hardship, Al-`Abbas agreed to take care of Ja`far, one of Abu Talib's sons, and Muhammad took care of Ali and moved him to his household. And so Ali was brought up in the most healthy moral climate under the care of Muhammad and his virtuous wife Khadijah!

Five years before this development, when Muhammad married Al- Sayyidah Khadijah, she gave him, as a gift, a slave boy called, Zaid. Muhammad freed him instantly and adopted him as a son in the manner of adoption in the pre-Islamic age. Henceforth he became known as Zaid Ibn Muhammad. As a matter of fact, Zaid was born a free person, a son of an Arab chief but he was captured in a night raid on his mother's camp by some unruly Bedouin group and sold as a slave boy in the market of Syria, from which a nephew of Al-Sayyidah Khadijah came and purchased him. His restless father, Harithah, who continued searching for his son was at last able to trace him in the household of Muhammad. Harithah offered to pay any price for his son to take him back with him. Muhammad raised no objection against the re-unification of the father and son, provided Zaid agreed to this re-union. Zaid who was happy to see his father again unhesitatingly preferred to remain with Muhammad!

And so, young Ali grew up as a child under the care of the noblest couple and as a sibling of Zaid and of their daughters Zainab, Ruqayyah, Ummu Kulthum and Fatima. (Giving of the name of an adopting parent to adopted children was later forbidden in Islam, and Zaid was henceforth called after his natural father).

With the Prophet's daughters and his adopted son, young Ali played and learned a great deal about the world surrounding him. When he became able to go around, he joined in the petty trade activities which was the pursuit of Muhammad himself. And when Ali approached the age of ten, he must have noticed that Muhammad often retired alone, and sometimes accompanied by Al-Sayyidah Khadijah, in a cave in a mountain called, Hira', where Muhammad spent hours, sometimes days, reflecting on the world and its amazing phenomena. Young Ali must have also been instilled with the virtues and perfect manners which dominated the climate of that noble home.

Chapter II
Ali as a Teenager

When Ali became ten years old, the Big Bang occurred! Muhammad Ibn Abd Allah Ibn Abd Al-Muttalib Ibn Hashim has received a Divine message from Heaven through the Archangel Jibril, "Gabriel," revealing to him the monotheistic creed calling for the worship of Allah alone and the abandonment of all atheistic superstitions and worship, and all unhealthy beliefs. Instead, the message called for upholding the creed of *tawhid*, for the cultivation of the virtues of charity, truthfulness, honesty, neighborliness and sympathy with the weak. It was then the year 610 AD.

Young Ali Embraces Islam:

At this early stage, Prophet Muhammad began to convey his message quietly and privately. If he chose then to invite for it openly and publicly, he would most probably have been met with a violent destructive reaction. So he confided his message first to Al-Sayyidah Khadijah who had known him inside out and appreciated his virtues and his merits. So she had no reason to doubt his claims or to reject his mission. On the contrary, she welcomed it wholeheartedly and embraced it warmly. Young Ali, just as a way of respect of his father, requested an opportunity to consult with Abu Talib when he was approached by the Prophet and invited to consider embracing the true faith. Yet, when he retired and had a moment of reflection, he saw no point or need for consultation. When Allah created him, He needed not to consult with Abu Talib, Ali reasoned. Even when he was still a baby in his mother's stomach, he must have been told, he did not let her bow before an idol. So he went up to the Prophet and declared the *Shahadah* words, namely: "I bear witness that there is no God but Allah, and that Muhammad is the Messenger of Allah." Young Ali was followed by Zaid. Abu Bakr, a close friend of the Prophet, nearly his age, and a successful Makkan merchant, was the fourth person to embrace the new religion. And thus, Khadijah, Ali, Zaid and Abu Bakr formed the earliest Muslim quadruple in Makkah.

Reaction to Public, Open Declaration of Islam:

The Prophet's first open declaration of Islam caused an earthquake that shook Makkah as if a large bomb had exploded over the heads of its inhabitants! They could not imagine that their gods, though they were idols formed from clay or wood or stone, could be so insulted as to be described as false and helpless. They awed them, worshipped them, prayed to them, and propitiated them. Those idols symbolized their religious authority and prestige and were recognized and respected all over Arabia. The annual pilgrimage, seasonal festivals and ceremonies, and the offerings and sacrifices made in their names brought the town prosperity, and many Makkans' livelihood depended on believing in them. Many Makkans saw Islam as a threat to their prosperity and was an insult to their honor and to their ancestors. So they rejected his call out-right, and resisted it by all possible means. Their offers to conduce him to give up his call, to pay him half the wealth of Makkah, to give him in marriage their prestigious girls, and to install him as King of Makkah failed to attract him. He was then subjected to abuses, insults and injuries, every thing that could hurt him short of slaying him.

That was the only thing they could not do to him, as it would provoke the anger of his powerful Hashimite clan and would displease his influential wife, Khadijah.

Retiring for Prayers with the Prophet:

In the early days of his Prophetic mission, the Messenger of Allah used to take young Ali away and pray together in one of those valleys outside Makkah, away from the eyes of Ali's father. However, they were once seen so doing by Abu Talib, Ali's father. Abu Talib asked the Prophet:

> "O my nephew! What is this religion you seem to be practicing?"

> "O my uncle!", the Prophet replied. "This is the religion of Allah and His Angels and His Apostles and the religion of our father Ibrahim. Almighty Allah has sent me as a Messenger to His creatures; and you, my uncle, are the first I should advise to embrace this faith and I invite you to follow its guidance. You are the fist person who should answer my call and help me in undertaking my mission."

> "O son of my brother!," Abu Talib responded; "I cannot abandon my ancestral religion and customs. Yet, by Allah, no one can hurt you as long as I live."

It is related that Abu Talib also once asked his own son, Ali,

> "What is this religion you seem to be practicing?"

> "O father," replied Ali, "I have believed in Allah and in the Messenger of Allah and accepted all that he has received from Heaven. I pray to Allah with him and follow his religion."

Abu Talib then told his son, Ali:

> "Since he leads you only to righteousness, follow him and keep close to him."

Persecution of the Muslims in Makkah:

When Abu Talib and Khadijah died within a short interval late in the tenth year of his call, the unbelievers intensified their persecution of the Prophet and those who embraced his religion.

Every day the Prophet came back home covered with dust and occasionally his body was bleeding from the stones thrown at him. Once he was almost strangled to death had it not been for the timely arrival of Abu Bakr at the place of the scene, and he rushed and released him from the grab of his assailant!

No doubt Ali must have been hit by some of the debris of this oppressive persecution, and he must have been a comforting factor at the Prophet's home, along with the Prophet's daughters who helped the Prophet wash away the dirt from his face and head on his return home!

The Prophet's Life Threatened:

When all the measures available to the enemies of Islam could not dissuade Muhammad and had failed to stop him from his persistent call for embracing the monotheistic creed and the abandonment of their useless idols and unbecoming beliefs, the Makkan inhabitants called Quraish, felt that they were left with no option except taking away Muhammad's life. After all, Abu Talib and Khadijah, his two powerful supporters had passed away. The surviving members of Muhammad's clan, they believed, would likely accept rich compensation for his life.

So the Quraish leadership planned a careful scheme to kill Muhammad in such a way that would make his clan incapable of asking for revenge and compel them to accept blood wealth (ransom) instead. So they arranged for a team of youth selected from all the Makkan clans except Banu Hashim, the clan to which the Prophet belonged, to go and lie in ambush by the Prophet's door step, with their swords unsheathed ready to strike him all at once as soon as he emerged from his door. In this way, they calculated, his blood would be scattered among all those clans, and Muhammad's clan would not be able to challenge them all for revenge.

Almighty Allah alerted the Prophet who planned at once to leave Makkah the same evening for good. His destination was Yathrib, 280 miles north of Makkah where he had already a strong support. The Yathribites who had met him secretly during the previous three-year pilgrimage seasons had invited him to emigrate to their town and pledged their full support and protection. Apparently the Quraish had a hunch of that plan, hence they had their eyes watching all tracks leading to Yathrib. Muhammad however had dedicated his life to the service and success of his mission, but the success of that mission depended on his survival until the new faith could stand on its own feet.

Young Ali Sleeps in the Prophet's Place:

Yet, how could the Prophet escape from Makkah unhurt when he was surrounded by his enemies, and here at his door step was this team of murderous young men awaiting in ambush for him? Even if he could pass miraculously safely through this ambushing party, how could he leave the whole town un-noticed should the awaiting party discover his departure from home before he had time to be away from the whole area? Once his escape from the house was discovered, the news about his departure would travel and spread around the city as fast as lightening. He needed time long enough for him to pick up Abu Bakr from his house and go to a hiding place far away enough from the city before the news about his departure could spread and an intensive search for him could be started.

Ali was the man of the hour. Youthful, energetic, daring and self-sacrificing, he agreed to sleep in the Prophet's place and to cover himself with the Prophet's mantle, knowing fully well that he was gravely exposing his life to real danger!

The Prophet, in the protection of Allah's eye, passed safely, and un-noticed, through the ambushing team who were blinded by a handful of dust thrown at them by the Prophet accompanied by a Qur'anic recitation: "And We have put a bar in front of them and a bar behind them, and further We have covered them up, so that they cannot see. (xxxvi, 9).

Trying hard as much as he could to keep away from the eyes of the people, the Prophet reached Abu Bakr's house at mid-day the next day, and soon they were both on their way to a hiding place in the opposite direction of Yathrib, their real final destination. Although the meetings of the Prophet with the Yathribites were held secretly, the Quraish seemed to have come to know about them and therefore as soon as they came to know about the Prophet's safe escape, their immediate search for him was in the direction of Yathrib.

The ambushing party, after a long waiting, became restless. They looked through, but it seemed to them that Muhammad was still there lying under that cover. Time and again, they looked through again and again but still the figure was there. At last, becoming too impatient, they decided to break into the house and strike that figure. Disturbed by their steps, Ali moved and uncovered his face as if he wanted to know what was happening. And here it was! Ali Ibn Abi Talib.........not Muhammad, their real target. Stunned and confused, and eager to rush to convey to their leaders the news of Muhammad's disappearance so that a quick thorough search for him could immediately be started, they left Ali alone unharmed! Soon, a rich reward was announced for anyone who could bring Muhammad back to Makkah alive or dead!

The Prophet Hides in a Cave:

Meantime Muhammad and Abu Bakr reached the foot of a mountain outside Makkah called Hira'. They climbed to a narrow cave in which they planned to hide. Abu Bakr went in first to ensure that there was nothing that might hurt the Prophet and filled the mouths of the holes inside except one which he could not block enough. He then requested the Prophet to come in and covered that opening with his own foot!

As soon as the Prophet, peace and blessings be upon him went inside the cave, spiders were sent by Almighty Allah and they wove housing webs that covered the entrance of the cave, making them look very old. A pigeon came and built a nest for herself and for her chicks at the lower edge of the cave's mouth.

The eager searching parties went in all directions, and the Arabs were a nation well known for their ability to trace the footsteps and correctly reach the whereabouts of their target. One of the searching parties traced the Prophet and Abu Bakr up to the foot of the mountain where they were hiding, and some of its members suggested to climb and investigate the condition of the cave closely; but they were discouraged by the scene of the spiders' nets and the presence of the pigeons and their undisturbed nest. Some of the party's members said that those spiders' nets looked older than Muhammad himself! As a matter of fact, Abu Bakr saw the feet of the members of that searching party from where he was, and in a worried tone told the Prophet:

"Should any one of them look from where his feet are, they would discover where we are!"

The Prophet, peace and blessings be upon him, reassured Abu Bakr:

"O Abu Bakr! They are truly so many and we are so few; but what do you think of two (persons) with Almighty Allah on their side."

The Prophet Cautiously Proceeds on the Hijrah Journey:

The searching party went away, and after a 3-day stay in the cave, the Prophet, peace and blessings be upon him, and Abu Bakr were on their way to Yathrib which the Prophet soon called Al-Madinah.

Had Imam Ali done nothing more than agree to go through that daring experience which was certainly instrumental in saving the Prophet's life and the protection of Islam, it would have been quite enough to raise him to the grade of the topmost few historical figures. And so, the Imam started the second decade of his life with embracing Islam and concluded it with his noble daring venture of exposing his life to a horrifying grave danger in order to save the Prophet's life and protect his religion!

Ali remained in Makkah for a while waiting for instruction from the Prophet after the Prophet's safe arrival at his destination. During this stay, he took care of the members of the Prophet's family who were still in Makkah and returned the valuable things which their Makkan owners had put under the trust of the Prophet. Although the unbelievers of Makkah rejected Islam and opposed the Prophet so vehemently, they still continued to trust him with things most dear to them as they correctly believed that he was the most trustworthy person they had ever known. So when the Prophet had to emigrate from Makkah, he handed over these trusts to the Imam, gave him the name of the owner of each item and asked him to return them each to its owner soon after his departure from Makkah. The Imam did as he was told faithfully and judiciously.

Chapter III

Ali's Emigration to Yathrib, "Al-Madinah"

Young Ali Leads a Party to Al-Madinah:

On his safe arrival at Qiba', an outskirt of Yathrib which the Prophet soon called, *Al-Madinah*, "The City," the Prophet, peace and blessings be upon him, sent a message to Imam Ali through someone called, Abu Waqid Al-Laithi, asking him to go and join him in Al-Madinah.

Taking along with him Al-Sayyidah Fatimah, the Prophet's youngest daughter, his own mother Fatimah Binti Asad, and Fatimah Binti Al-Zubair Ibn Abd Al-Muttalib, Ali's paternal aunt, as well as Ayman, the Imam proceeded on his way to Al-Madinah accompanied by Abu Waqid who was driving the riding beasts somewhat too fast. Imam Ali told him: "Slowly, slowly, Aba Waqid. The ladies cannot withstand this much hardship." Abu Waqid said, "I am afraid we might be chased by the enemies!", to which the Imam responded: "Be not afraid, O Aba Waqid!"

Abu Waqid's fears were justified! Half way during the journey, they were overtaken by a party of hooded knights who ordered them to stop, to let the camels kneel and to let the women dismount! The daring Imam refused to do so defiantly and fearlessly. The leader of that hooded party struck Ali with his sword, but the Imam pushed away that sword with his powerful arm and, with the other hand struck that aggressor with his own sword cutting him into two halves. Turning to the other members of the party of hooded knights and chanting the words, in a poetic form:

> "Let alone him who is struggling on the right path
> I have made an oath to worship none but the One God!"

the Imam scared them and, afraid for their own lives, they ran away leaving the body of their friend lying in the open desert to feed its vultures!

The Imam with the noble ladies and Abu Waqid proceeded less fearful on their way to the Prophet, peace and blessings be upon him. While they were still on the way, they were joined by a party of believers who were ill-treated and despised by the Makkans in view of their modest roots, including Umm Ayman, one of the wet nurses of the Prophet who suckled him as a newly born baby before he was trusted to Halimah of Banu Saud, and who joined him and his mother, Al-Sayyidah Aminah when the three of them paid a visit to his father's uncles in Yathrib. Then the Prophet was just six years old. We may also recall here that his mother died on the way back, and Ummu Ayman took him and delivered him safely to his grandfather! So, Ali's party travelled together, interrupting their journey by saying their prayers whenever time for a prayer became due. It was in that context that the following Qur'anic passage was revealed:

> "Verily, in the creation of the heavens and the earth, and the alteration of Night and Day, there are signs for those of understanding. Those who celebrate the praise of Allah standing, and lying on their sides, and contemplating over the (wonders of) the creation of the heavens and the earth, reflecting: 'O our Lord! Not in vain have You created (all) this! Glory be to You. Grant us salvation from the punishment in the Fire. Our Lord, anyone whom you let enter into the Fire, surely You cover him with shame, and never will wrong-doers find any helpers! Our Lord! We have heard the call of one calling (us) to Faith, and we have believed. Our Lord! So forgive our sins, blot out from us our iniquities, and let us die being along with the righteous. Our Lord! Grant us that which You promised us through Your Messengers and save us from shame on the Day of Judgment. You indeed never break Your promise. And their Lord granted them what

they pleaded for, answering them: 'Never shall I cause to be lost the deed of any of you, male or female. You are members, one of another. So, those who have immigrated, having been expelled from their own homes, and been caused to sustain harm on account of My cause, and fought and been killed I shall certainly blot out their iniquities and let them dwell in Gardens beneath which rivers flow—a reward from Allah. And Allah has with Him the best of all rewards." (Chapter II, verses 190-5)

Safe Arrival of Imam Ali's Party in Al-Madinah:

When the party arrived in Al-Madinah, the Prophet, peace and blessings be upon him, welcomed them wholeheartedly. He kissed Fatimah, hugged her, and holding Ali's hand, said:

"This is my brother. He is the one who will inherit my knowledge, He will be, along with my daughter, Fatimah, in my company in Paradise!"

Chapter IV

The Third Decade

This was perhaps the most blessed and the most fertile stage in the life of the Imam. Throughout this decade Imam Ali remained close to the Prophet benefiting from his blessings and drinking deeply from his knowledge. This continguinity which was based not only on blood relationship but also on mutual love and admiration, was further enhanced as we shall see, by Ali's marriage to a bride who was the closest person to the heart of the Prophet; namely, his daughter Fatimah Al-Zahra', "The Fresh-Flower-like Shining Creature."

In view of the multi-various aspects of this stage in the life of our great Imam, and in order to be more clear in our presentation, this chapter is divided into sub-chapters each of which appears under a relevant title.

The Imam's Involvement, Serving the Prophet as a Scribe:

As a leading member of the choice of the early community of Islam, and in view of his sharp intelligence and wide knowledge, Imam Ali was deeply involved in all important developments in the affairs of the state newly set up in Al-Madinah despite his young age. For example, he was one of the team of a few trusted with the task of writing down the text of the Holy Qur'an. Whenever a passage of the Holy Qur'an was revealed to the Prophet, peace and blessings be upon him, it was written down on the order of the Prophet by a member or members of that team who happened to be then available. By the time of the death of the Prophet, the entire text of the Holy Qur'an which was deeply engraved in the Companions' memories, was also completely preserved in writing. As we may recall, all written Qur'anic pieces were collected by Abu Bakr, the First Caliph, who kept them in his custody until shortly before his death. He then handed them over to Umar Ibn Al-Khattab who was designated to succeed him; and Umar, in turn, handed them over to his daughter Hafsah, a widow of the Prophet, while he was struggling with death after he was stabbed with a poisoned sword, very unfortunately! These Qur'anic records remained with Al-Sayyidah Hafsah until it was time for them to be duplicated for distribution for the guidance of Muslims in the various provinces. This happened during the reign of Sayyidina Uthman Ibn Affan who withdrew them from her and had them duplicated carefully by a committee chaired by Zaid Ibn Thabit, who had chaired the committee which had successfully collected and put together those Qur'anic documents during the reign of Abu Bakr, may Almighty Allah be pleased with them all.

United with the Prophet in a Special Brotherly Tie:

Another indication that shows that Imam Ali dwelt in a special corner in the heart of the Prophet was that, from amongst all the Companions, Imam Ali was united in a special brotherhood tie with the Prophet. The story goes like this: During the early part of the Prophet's stay in Al-Madinah, the Prophet, peace be upon him, set a special bond of unity between each two members of the Muslim community, often one from the Makkan Immigrants and another from the Madinese group: *Al-Ansar*, "The Supporters." This was apparently in order to further strengthen the bond of unity and to make life easier, especially for *Al-Muhajirin*, "The Immigrants." Imam Ali then went up to the Prophet with tears in his eyes, and asked: "With whom have I been united, O Messenger of Allah?" The Prophet, peace and blessings be upon him, told him:

"You, (Ali), are my brother in this world and in the Hereafter!"

Ali's Marriage to Fatimah:

The close relationship uniting the Prophet and the Imam was further enhanced by the marriage of the Imam to Al-Sayyidah Fatimah, the Prophet's daughter who was the closest person to the heart of her father. Whenever she approached, the Prophet stood up, hugged her and kissed her. Once Al-Sayyidah `A'ishah remarked:

"O Messenger of Allah! Whenever Fatimah came, you kiss her so passionately as if you were licking honey!"

The Prophet, peace and blessings be upon him, explained:

"On the night I was taken away (to Jerusalem and then to heaven,) Jibril, Gabriel, led me enter Paradise and gave me (samples) of all its fruits to eat. Their juices penetrated into my body, and it was then that Khadijah begot Fatima. So whenever I crave for the sweet odor of these fruits I kiss Fatimah, which brings me back to the sweet smell of thesefruits."

The Four Most Meritorious Women:

Whatever the scholars might argue about the authenticity of this hadith, it reflects in a sweet manner the immense degree of the Prophet's love of Fatimah. It is agreed, however, that Fatimah is counted among the four most meritorious women of all times; namely: Al-Sayyidah Maryam Binti (daughter of) Imran (mother of Jesus); Fatimah Binti Muhammad, peace and blessings be upon him, Al-Sayyidah Khadijah Binti Khuwailid (first wife of the Prophet, peace and blessings be upon him), and Asiyah (the Pharaoh's wife who successfully pleaded with her husband, the Pharaoh of Egypt, to spare the life of the infant Moses after picking him up from the River Nile when he was found floating near the wall of the royal palace).

According to another opinion, Al-Sayyidah `A'ishah Binti Abi Bakr, the Prophet's wife, replaces Asiyah in that list. Some one listed these four in a poetic style for easy remembering, saying:

فضلى النساء بنت عمران ففاطمة ∴ خديجة ثم من قد برأ الله

It means: "The (four) most meritorious women (are) Binti `Imran (Maryam), then Fatimah (Binti Muhammad), Khadijah (Binti Khuwailid), then she whom Allah declared her innocence (from the false accusation unfairly made against her by certain hypocrites, and the Holy Qur'an asserted her innocence in Chapter xxiv verses 20-21), namely, `A'ishah.

Proceeding of the Marriage Ceremony:

The story of the marriage of the Imam to Al-Sayyidah Fatimah was related by Anas Ibn Malik who was in the service of the Prophet, peace and blessings be upon him. On arrival of the Prophet in Al-Madinah at the time of the Hijrah, this Anas was ten years old. His mother took him by his hand and pleaded to the Prophet, peace and blessings be upon him, to take Anas in his service. He welcomed the offer, and Anas remained in the household of the Prophet for the rest of the Prophet's life. Anas later said:

> "I served the Prophet, peace and blessings be upon him, for ten years. He never blamed me over something I did, why I had done it, or on account of something I did not do why I neglected it."

This lucky Companion relates the story of Imam Ali's marriage to Al-Sayyidah Fatimah in the following words:

> "Once while I was with the Prophet, he went into a stance, as used to happen when he received revelation from Heaven.

> "When he recovered, he said: O Anas! Do you know what message I have just received from Almighty Allah?

Jibril (the Archangel Gabriel), conveyed to me a commandment from Allah that I should give Fatimah away in marriage to Ali. So go and invite Abu Bakr, Umar, Uthman, Talhah and Al-Zubair, and an equal number of the Ansar, (Helpers, the Madinese).' So I went away and did as I was commanded. When they all gathered, the Messenger of Allah, peace and blessings be upon him, delivered the following address:

"Praise be to Allah Who deserves all gratitude on account of His favors. He alone deserves to be worshipped for His overwhelming power. His authority is to be obeyed. He is sought as a refuge from His punishment. His commands are executed on the earth and in heavens which are all His. He created all creatures through His power, and favored them with His judgments, and strengthened them with His religion, and blessed them with His Messenger Muhammad, peace and blessings be upon Him.

"Verily Allah has made marriage a (measure for legitimate) descent and an obeyed command, and a just rule and an all-embracing blessing, whereby nuptial binding links are forged. So Almighty Allah says (in the Holy Qur'an): `It is He (Allah) Who has created man from water then has made it relationships of lineages and marriage, for your Lord has power (over all things).'

"Allah's commands agree with His predestination, and His predestination leads to His decrees. And for every predestined thing there is a decree and each decreed thing has an appointed time,

"Allah blots out or confirms whatever He pleases; and with Him is the Mother of the Book.

"Verily Allah has commanded me to offer Fatimah in marriage to Ali, and you are my witness that I am marrying Fatimah to Ali on the payment of a dower amounting to four hundred *mithqals* (600 *dirhams*) of silver, if he should agree (to this) in accordance with the prevailing customs and the obtaining obligations. May Almighty Allah bless their union and grant them prosperity, and may He bless them with honorable offspring and make their descendants keys to mercy and sources of wisdom and a refuge for the ummah. So I seek Allah's forgiveness for myself and for you."

On the Prophet's order, a plate of dates was placed before the guests.

It is interesting that all this happened in Ali's absence, as he was away running an errand for the Prophet, peace and blessings be upon him. On Ali's return, while the guests were helping themselves from the dates, the Prophet smilingly told Ali:

"O Ali. Verily Allah has commanded me to offer you Fatimah in marriage, and I have married her to you on the payment, as a dower, of four hundred *mithqals* of silver."

Ali responded:

"I (gratefully) accept (the offer), O Messenger of Allah."
Ali then prostrated in gratitude to Allah.

When Ali raised his head from prostration, the Prophet, peace and blessings be upon him, said, addressing Ali,

"May Allah grant you both His blessings. May He make you (both) happy and may He bring forth from you many noble offspring!"

Ali and Fatimah were wed about two months from then, and they lived happily ever after. The Prophet, peace and blessings be upon him, arranged for their residence to be close to his, so he could see them often. It is related that the Prophet, peace and blessings be upon him, once heard that Imam Ali was planning to marry the daughter of Amr Ibn Hisham, his archenemy, who led the Makkan opposition against him and whom he had nicknamed Abu Jahl, "Father of Ignorance." Abu Jahl led the army of unbelievers on the Day of Badr, and was slain in that battle.

On hearing of the rumor about Ali's intention to marry Abu Jahl's daughter, the Prophet, peace be upon him, was displeased. He mounted the pulpit and delivered a sermon in which he said:

"Verily I do not wish to make something lawful unlawful, or that which is unlawful lawful, but the daughter of the Messenger of Allah cannot live with the daughter of the enemy of Allah under the same roof."

Children Begotten through That Blessed Marriage:

Ali's marriage to Fatimah produced six children: Al-Hasan (born mid-Ramadan, 3 A.H), and Al-Husain (born 5th Sha`ban 4 AH) whom the Prophet described as the most noble among the youth in Paradise. In addition, Fatimah gave birth to Muhsin who died young, Ummu Kulthum, Ruqayyah, and Zainab. The Prophet loved his grandchildren very deeply. On their birth, he made the `aqiqah* and performed the *sunnah* custom of rubbing the baby's palate with his noble tongue. He used to carry them and to play with them, and even allowed them to mount his back while leading the prayers in the mosque. The Prophet once in his prayer extended the *sujud,* "prostration". On completing his prayers, he explained to the congregation that he was mounted by Umamah (his granddaughter from Zainab), and he waited in his *sujud* (in order not to disturb her), until she dismounted! May Almighty Allah bestow all His blessings upon His great, noble Messenger who was so tenderhearted and so clement up to that degree in spite of the weight of his tremendous responsibilities!

The Imam Undertakes Missions on Behalf of the Prophet:

The Prophet's trust and confidence in the Imam and recognition of his un-surpassed erudition, were reflected in the

Prophet's selection of the Imam to undertake important missions on his behalf. One such mission took place during the pilgrimage season in the 9th year after the Hijrah. Abu Bakr had gone already to Makkah as *Amir Al-Hajj*, "Prince, (Commandant) in charge of the pilgrimage season." It happened then that a Qur'anic text was revealed declaring the release of the Prophet and his community from the terms and commitments made in agreements concluded earlier with the polytheists. Of course, by then almost the entire inhabitants of the Arabian peninsula had embraced Islam and committed themselves to its tenets; so those earlier commitments had become of no real significance. Imam Ali was sent and instructed to read out that text himself unto the large gathering of the pilgrims himself. And he did as instructed. The early part of that Qur'anic text reads as follows:

> "A declaration of immunity from Allah and His Messenger to the polytheists with whom you have contracted mutual alliances:

> "Go you, then, for four months, backwards and forwards (as you will), throughout the land, but know you that you cannot frustrate Allah (by your falsehood), but that Allah will cover with shame those who reject Him.

> "And an announcement from Allah and His Messenger to the people assembled on the day of the great pilgrimage—that Allah and His Messenger (hereby) dissolve (treaty) obligations concluded with the polytheists. So, if you repent, it will be best for you; but if you should turn away, know you that you cannot frustrate Allah. And proclaim to the unbelievers a painful punishment which is awaiting them;

> "But agreements remain valid, which were made with polytheists who have not subsequently encroached upon you in any way nor did aid anyone against you. So fulfill your agreements with them to the end of their term, for indeed Allah loves the righteous.

"Yet, when the sacred months are over, then (fight and) kill the polytheists wherever you encounter them, and seize them, and surround them, and lie in wait for them in every military stratagem. If, however, they should repent and regularly observe the (daily) prayers, and give out the zakat, then leave them alone. Verily Allah is Oft-Forgiving and Most Merciful.

"And should one of the polytheists plead to you for asylum, grant it to him, so that he may hear the speech of Allah; and then help him go to a place where he can be secure. That is because they are a people without knowledge." IX:1-6.

It was suggested to the Prophet that Abu Bakr should read out that declaration, but the Prophet retorted: "Only one from my household shall do so."

Another mission the Imam was asked by the Prophet to undertake on his behalf was to the Yemen, in the year 10 A.H. He was to teach these people the text of the Holy Qur'an, the tenets of the faith, and to settle their disputes. The Imam relates that when he was asked to undertake that mission he complained to the Prophet, peace and blessings be upon him, saying:

"O Messenger of Allah! How can I be asked to go to judge between those people when I am still so young and with no experience in the court procedure?"

The Imam relates that the Prophet then patted gently on Ali's chest and that he heard him then praying:

"O Almighty Allah! Guide his heart aright and make his tongue firm."

The Imam added:

"By Him Who split open the grain, since then I have not hesitated or doubted when settling disputes.".

Chapter V

The Imam's Unmatched Valor

On the Eve of the Hijrah:

Reference has been made to the Imam's daring acceptance to sleep in the place of the Prophet, peace and blessings be upon him, on the night of the Prophet's planned departure from Makkah to Al-Madinah, the historic Hijrah journey. It was not merely a matter of courage and fearlessness, but also the spirit of self-sacrificing. The Imam must have expected that the ambushing party of youth were most likely to strike him at once with their unsheathed swords as soon they uncover his face and realize they had missed their aim, on account of his role in misleading them. Yet he agreed to take this grave risk without any hesitation.

On the Way to Al-Madinah:

We have also learned how the Imam was able, almost single-handedly to overcome the hooded party of knights who chased and intercepted the Imam's small party who included three distinguished ladies when they were on their way emigrating to join the Prophet in Al-Madinah. The hooded knights were so frightened that they had to run away leaving the body of their dead leader poorly lying in the open desert—and the Imam's little party proceeded safely on their way to the Prophet, peace and blessings be upon him. On arrival in Al-Madinah, Al-Sayyidah Fatimah stayed with her father and his wife Sawdah Binti Zam`an. When she was married, she moved to her nuptial home and stayed with the Imam quite happily. Very rarely did some tiffs occur. On one of these incidents, Imam Ali left the house and stayed in the Mosque. On hearing about it, the Prophet went to see the Imam to settle the matter, but found the young Imam asleep with his bare back covered with dust. The Prophet, peace and blessings be upon him, began to remove the dust away from his back, saying: "Wake up Aba Turab! Wake up Aba Turab!" Ever since then, the title Abu Turab, "one covered with dust", became the dearest name to the Imam himself. Al-Sayyidah Fatimah, who died six months after her great father, begot six children, three sons: Al-Hasan, Al-Husain and Muhsin; and three daughters: Ummu Kulthum, Zainab and Ruqayyah. Muhsin and Ruqayya died young.

On the Day of Badr:

During the period of the Islamic call in Makkah, almost thirteen years, the Prophet and his few Companions responded to the savage persecution they suffered at the hands of the polytheists, with patience and forbearance. Forceful resistance could very well have dealt a death blow to the Islamic call in its infancy. In Al-Madinah, the situation became different. There was a state, an organization, and a rapid expansion of the faith. So there was a need to protect the integrity of the state and the life and the interests of its citizens. It was also necessary to carry the *da`wah*, "the Islamic call," to the ears of all peoples, far and wide, and to remove at any cost all prejudicial blocks from its way. Let us now see what happened, and examine the role played by our great Imam in that tremendous effort.

The Prophet's successful migration to Al-Madinah, thus escaping from the claws of his Makkan enemies and becoming able to practice his religion freely, gaining more followers and steadily growing in strength at the cost of their polytheistic falsehood, inflated the anger of the Makkan polytheists and made them more determined not only to destroy him but also to eliminate his religion and all his supporters. A series of military battles ensued in which the Imam's prowess, acumen, unmatched courage and superior military capabilities revealed themselves and played a leading role in the defense and survival of Islam. Let's now quote some examples of his heroic deeds.

During the second year of the Hijrah, in Ramadan, the unbelievers decided to launch a major attack on Al-Madinah. They had already, since the Prophet left Makkah, mounted a series of mean raids against Al-Madinah, destroying properties, burning fields, and running away with whatever they could grab from the wealth of the town. This time they marched with a large, well organized army determined to erase the town. On hearing of this development, and the Prophet had always been keeping an eye on Makkah and the movements of its atheists so that he might not be taken by surprise, he quickly organized his men and moved to intercept the enemies. The two camps met at *Badr*, hence this battle is called, "The Battle of Badr."

When the two parties camped against each other, three men emerged from the polytheistic camp: Utbah Ibn Rabi`ah (a proud wealthy polytheist), his son Al-Walid, and his brother Shaibah. Utbah cried:

"O Muhammad! Let three men of our calibre from amongst your men venture to fight us!"

Three Madinese Companions rushed out in response, wearing their armor. When Utbah came to know they were Madinese, he refused to fight them and said he wanted three Makkan Quraishites. The Prophet, peace and blessing be upon him called:

"O Ali: Rise! O Hamzah: Rise! O Ubaidah (Ibn Al-Harith Ibn Abd Al-Muttalib): Rise!"

When these three gallant men approached, Utbah commanded his son, Al-Walid: "Go and finish Ali". Al-Walid tried to strike Ali with a blow, but missed. Ali returned the blow with a stroke that blew off Al-Walid's left arm, followed by another one that threw him dead on the ground. Meantime, Al-Hamzah had slain Utbah; then he and Ali turned to help the aging Ubaidah and slew Shaibah. It was a good start and the day ended in a brilliant victory for Islam. Although Muslims were outnumbered, (just about three hundred against about one thousand), the Muslim army routed their enemies, slaying seventy of them, including some of their top men, and capturing seventy war prisoners who were later released on payment of ransoms. The Muslims were exceedingly motivated. They were quite ready to lay their lives in sacrifice for their religion!

Imam Ali used to recall his fighting with Al-Walid Ibn Utbah and the shining colors of a wedding ring in his hand from which he gathered that Al-Walid had been newly wed! From amongst the seventy polytheists slain at Badr, Imam Ali was credited with overcoming twenty-one of them!

On the Day of Uhud:

In the famous battle at *Uhud*, a mountain just outside Al-Madinah, which took place in the third year of the Hijrah when the Quraish launched a fierce attack on the Muslims to revenge their defeat at Badr, the Imam's role was also as great. Muslims were about to win another decisive victory, but the chance was lost as a result of the unwise move of the Muslim archers against the instructions of the Prophet. This led to a great confusion in the Muslim lines. Imam Ali was one of the few who stood firm to protect the Prophet until the enemies had to run away. The Imam helped his wife Al-Sayyidah Fatimah wash away her father's wounds and carried water from far for that purpose.

The loss to the polytheists in that battle at Uhud amounted to twenty-two of their best warriors of whom seven were slain by our Imam, including Talhah Ibn Abi Talhah, the carrier of the flag of the polytheists on that day who boastfully came out of their camp shouting:

> "O friends of Muhammad! You claim that those of you who fall in battle are swiftly sent by Allah to Paradise; and those of us slain by you are immediately sent to Hell. So let any of you dare to come to fight me in order to go quickly to Paradise or send (him) to Hell."

Imam Ali, confident in Allah's protection, emerged, shouting at him:

"By Allah! I shall not leave you until I have sent you with this sword (in my hand) to the Hell Fire!"

A duel started in the battle ground; and, with a single hit the young Imam severed Talha's legs, thus felling him to the ground bleeding profusely! Seeing the Imam raising his sword to finish him completely, Talhah pleaded to the Imam: *karrama Allahu wajhahu*, "May Almighty Allah let his face shine with honor." By Allah and our blood bond, please have mercy upon me!"

The Imam left him alone and returned to the Muslim camp. Umar Ibn Al-Khattab reproached the Imam, saying:

"Why haven't you finished him off?"

The Imam quietly replied:

"He uncovered his `awrah, his private parts, and I had to turn away. Anyhow he is dying!"

It is asserted that Imam Ali never seen the `awrah of anybody, not even his own. Therefore, when his name is mentioned, it provokes the recitation of the prayer words *karrama Allahu wajhahu:* "May Allah let his face shine with honor!"

During the Battle of the Ditch:

Imam Ali's military brilliance was even more vividly demonstrated during the battle known as The Battle of the Allies, when almost all the evil forces joined hands with Quraish who were seriously determined to destroy Islam and its town. An army of ten thousand fighters led by Abu Sufyan, the leader of Quraish since Abu Jahl was slain on the day of Badr, and including a fair number of the fearful warriors from the desert tribe of Ghatafan, marched to destroy Al-Madinah late in the fourth year of Al-Hijrah. In that grave situation, and after consultation with his Companions, the Prophet, peace and blessings be upon him decided to remain in the town to defend it from within and to dig a ditch to protect the vulnerable part of the boundary of the town, following the advice of his Companion, Salman of Persia. The situation was made worse by an agreement concluded between the Quraish party and the Jews of Al-Madinah who treacherously undertook to launch an attack upon the Muslims simultaneously when the Allies would start to strike. However, when the Allied army arrived and encountered the ditch, they were frustrated. They had to camp at the external edge of the ditch facing the much smaller Muslim army camping at the other side, to plan what to do in the circumstances.

To cut the story short, the siege was ultimately lifted as a result of the Allies' frustration owing to a long, protracted siege, their betrayal by the Jews, their heavy losses in duels fought by Muslim warriors like the Imam, and a strong, very cold night winds which uprooted their tents, threw away their belongings and destroyed their morale. The town was miraculously saved and Islam survived intact!

Let us quote one example of the performance of the Imam in that awesome battle. A famous warrior from the Ghatafan tribe called `Amr Ibn Abd Wadd came out and challenged the Muslim army for a duel. Imam Ali requested the Prophet to let him respond to `Amr's challenge. In view of the reputation of `Amr and his concern for young Ali's life, the Prophet, peace and blessings be upon him, did not grant Ali permission. `Amr, deceived by failing to get a response from the Muslim party became more conceited and more arrogant. He shouted in a poetical form the proud words:

"I have lost my voice urging your camp for a duel!
Where is your courage, and where is your spirit of sacrificing?"

Young Ali, emerging from the Muslim camp, having successfully secured the Prophet's approval after repeated pleading, his head wrapped with the Prophet's own turban, shouted at `Amr Ibn Abd Wadd, chanting:

"Be not in a hurry; here I am to take up your challenge,
"Able and truthful, and eager to see women wailing over your death,
"By a skillful fatal blow that shall be forever remembered!"

The two great warriors descended into the ditch and faced each other. The Imam tried at first to reason with him, saying:

"I understand you had committed yourself publicly to honor any invitation extended to you on behalf of a noble cause; and I now invite you to embrace Islam and to yield to Allah and to His Messenger!"

`Amr, who was accompanied by his son, Hanbal, arrogantly declined the invitation.

"In this case," the Imam told him, "You are welcome to a fight!"

`Amr who then had come to know who his challenger was, told him:

"Abu Talib, your father, was a good friend of mine and I do not wish to slay the son of a friend of mine."

to which young Ali responded:

"But I do wish to slay you!"

Angrily, `Amr dismounted, and so did Ali. A fierce battle ensued, tensely watched by the two armies from above. At last, with a powerful stoke by the Imam, `Amr was thrown onto the ground motionless. Then the Imam turned to Hanbal and finished him. Relieved and exhilarated, the Muslims chanted the words of *takbir*, expressing their gratitude to Almighty Allah for their deliverance and the safety of their town. The polytheists withdrew badly distraught and humiliated!

Writing down Al-Hudaibiyah Agreement:

It will be beyond the scope of this modest work to attempt to exhaust the list of the glorious military successes on behalf of Islam and its defense during the life time of the Prophet and under his command and guidance, and the role played by the Imam therein. We therefore conclude this discussion with a brief reference to some of his performance during the battle of *Khaibar*, a group of fertile oases, which took place in *Safar*, the second month of the seventh Hijrah year. This was shortly after the peace treaty concluded between the Prophet, peace and blessings be upon him, and the Quraish of Makkah at Al-Hudaibiyah, just outside the territory of Makkah on the way to Jeddah. The text of the treaty was written down by Imam Ali as dictated by the Prophet, peace and blessings be upon him. The text of the treaty was to begin with the words:

"This is what has been agreed to between Muhammad Rasul Allah and The Quraish——etc."

`Amr Ibn Sahl, representing Quraish objected to the use of the phrase, Rasul Allah, "The Messenger of Allah", on the ground that this subject was the disputed issue. The Prophet agreed to have that phrase deleted and replaced by the words, "Muhammad Ibn Abd Allah." When he was advised to delete the words, *Rasul Allah*, Imam Ali refused and said:

"By Him Who has sent you with the Truth, I shall never delete it."

The Prophet, peace and blessings be upon him, then asked the Imam to show him the place of that phrase, and deleted it with his own hand saying to the Imam, "One day you will go through a similar experience."

When the Prophet, peace and blessings be upon him began his march towards Khaibar in Muharram 7th Hijrah year, Imam Ali led the Muslim forces carrying the Prophet's white flag. In the month of Safar, having reached their destination, the Muslim forces who had been engaged in duels, began to assault the Jewish fortifications, *husun*, one after the other. The Imam, of course, had his effective part in overcoming these fortifications.

One day, the Prophet, peace and blessings be upon him, sent Abu Bakr to deal with one of these fortifications; he returned at the end of the day unsuccessfully exhausted! The following day he sent Umar Ibn Al-Khattab with a contingent to open the same fort; but the result was no better! The Prophet then said:

> "Allah willing, I shall give the flag tomorrow to a man who loves Allah and His Messenger and who never retreats."

Many of the Prophet's Companions craved to be that person. The following morning, however, the Prophet sent for Ali to come to see him. The Prophet was told that Ali was suffering from opthamalia. The Prophet yet insisted on seeing the Imam. When Ali came, the Prophet rubbed his eyes gently with his finger wet with his blessed saliva; and the Imam was fully cured. The Prophet then ordered him:

"Take this flag and fight. Allah will open the way for you! Should Allah guide one person through you, it will be better for you than red camels."

Let us listen to the story about what then happened as related by Abu Rafi`, one of the Prophet's freed men who witnessed that event:

> "We proceeded forth under the command of Ali Ibn Abi Talib, may Almighty Allah be pleased with him, when the Messenger of Allah sent him holding his (the Prophet's) flag. Once he approached that fort, its inhabitants came out and fought him hard. A Jew hit his shield with a powerful blow and the shield dropped from Ali's hand. Ali immediately picked up a huge gate door that was lying closeby and used it as a shield. Ali continued to fight with the door in his hand until the enemies were defeated and the fort was open widely to Islam. After Ali

dropped that door, eight of us, including myself, tried just to turn it over, we could not!"

So another major success for Islam was owed to Imam Ali, and achieved by his perseverance and stamina!

On the Day of the Conquest of Makkah:

When the Prophet, peace and blessings be upon him, was on his way at the head of 10,000 men marching upon Makkah, whose inhabitants, the Quraish, had violated the terms of the Hudaibiyah agreement, of course, Imam Ali was among his devoted generals. However, the Prophet had sought to make this conquest as bloodless as possible and therefore he kept his destination as secret as long as could be. The Muslim forces were to go into the town from different entrances one of which was called The Gate of Kuda'. The leader of the contingent which was to enter through that gate was Sa`d Ibn `Ubadah, the head of the Khazrajite tribe of Al-Madinah. He was heard shouting excitedly:

"Today is the (chance) of a smiting battle!"

When the Prophet, peace and blessings be upon him, heard of this, he told Imam Ali:

"Go and take the flag from him, and try to overtake him. Keep the flag in your hand, and be the first to enter the city (from that entrance)."

Imam Ali did as he was told.

As we know, the Prophet, peace and blessings be upon him, had declared an amnesty, according to which a safe passage would be granted to any Makkan who might seek refuge in the sanctuary around the Ka`bah. So people rushed to that sanctuary, called Al-Haram and gathered there waiting to learn about their future as it might be determined by the Prophet.

Sitting quietly and fearfully, they watched Muhammad Ibn Abd Allah, the Messenger of Allah, then the most powerful man, enter into the area, on the back of his she-camel, lowering his head in modesty to Allah and murmuring words of prayers and praise of Almighty Allah. When he became close to the Ka`bah they saw him dismounting and then making the tawaf around the Ka`bah, concluded by two rak`ats of prayers. The Prophet then asked Imam Ali to get the Ka`bah door key from `Uthman Ibn Talhah, from the family who had been the custodian of the Ka`bah from early times. When `Uthman hesitated, Imam Ali twisted his hand, took the key, and the Ka`bah door was wide open to welcome the Prophet, peace and blessings be upon him. The Prophet entered the Ka`bah having ordered the Imam to break all the idols installed around the Ka`bah and asked Bilal Ibn Rabah to recite the adhan from the top of the Ka`bah. The fearful people of Quraish, while their hearts were beating faster and faster, listened to Bilal chanting the words:

"Allahu Akbar. Allahu Akbar. I bear witness that there is no god but Allah, ... I bear witness that Muhammad is the Messenger of Allah ...", and at the same time watching their idols pushed to the ground, one after another by the Imam's powerful hand, disintegrating helplessly into scattered small pieces of stone!

More and more eager to learn of their fate, they saw the Prophet, peace and blessings be upon him, emerging from the door of the Ka`bah. He stepped out and, standing on its step facing the huge gathering of the Makkans, the Prophet, in a calm serene voice, asked them:

"O people of Quraish. What do you expect me to do to you?"

"What to expect from a noble brother who is the son of a noble brother." They replied:

"You may all go. You are all free," the Prophet graciously declared.

That was the noble verdict of a noble man. No mass slaughter. No enslavement, and no punishment whatsoever. All their war crimes, all their aggression, and their severe persecution of the Prophet prior to the Hijrah were generously forgiven! No doubt they were all happily relieved, and shortly afterwards, they voluntarily converted to Islam!

The Prophet, peace and blessings be upon him, remained in the area of Makkah for a few days after the accomplishment of the conquest, alternating between the Haram Mosque and a tent pitched for him outside the town.

Once while the Prophet, peace and blessings be upon him, was resting in the Mosque, Imam Ali went up to him and suggested that the custodianship of the Ka`bah and the obligation of providing water for the pilgrims be transferred to the family of Hashim, (the family to which the Prophet and the Imam belonged). The Prophet preferred to let that trust remain where it had been, and sent for `Uthman Ibn Talhah. The Prophet gave him back the Ka`bah key, and said:

"Today is a day of kindness and faithfulness!"

As soon as the town surrendered, while Imam Ali was still wearing his armor, he heard that two polytheists were hiding in the home of his sister who was nicknamed Umm Hani'. They were related to her husband, Hubairah, who had run away from Makkah on hearing of the Muslims' marching on the town. Imam Ali went to his sister's house to chase those two men, still wearing his armor. Umm Hani', however, refused to surrender those two men to the Imam. She hid them behind a closed door. When her pleading to her brother on behalf of those two men proved to be of no avail, Umm Hani' ran away to the Prophet's tent. The Prophet happened to be having ablution behind a curtain held for him by his daughter, Al-Sayyidah Fatimah. When he finished his ablution, the Prophet, peace and blessings be upon him, asked her:

"O Umm Hani'. What can we do for you?"

She informed him of the two men who Imam Ali wanted to surrender to him. The Prophet, peace and blessings be upon him, told her:

> "O Umm Hani'. We protect those you protect, and grant a safe passage to all those you wish to be safe."

May Almighty Allah bestow all his blessings upon you, Messenger of Allah!

The Prophet Visits Umm Hani':

It may be relevant to mention here in the context of the conquest of Makkah the story of a visit paid by the Prophet to the home of his female cousin in Makkah, called: Ramlah Bint Abi Talib, and nicknamed Umm Hani'. In his young age, the Prophet used to like this cousin of his, and he asked for her hand before his marriage to Khadijah. Her father, Abu Talib who preferred an exonymous marriage, disagreed, and the Prophet married Khadijah, as we know. On the day of the conquest of Makkah, the Prophet paid Umm Hani' a visit. He asked whether she had some food to eat. She said that she had just a piece of bread and a drop of vinegar. The Prophet said:

> "How good vinegar is as an appetizer!"

So, Umm Hani' brought him the vinegar and the piece of bread. Imagine! A great triumphant leader, on the day of his most glorious conquest, feasts himself on a piece of bread and a drop of vinegar! Seeing that Ramlah's husband had run away, and anyhow Islam had separated and released Umm Hani' from her nuptial bond with Hubairah for good, the Prophet renewed his proposal to her in marriage. She said:

> "No, O Messenger of Allah. If I should marry you now, I shall be bound either to fail in my obligations to you as my husband or in my attention due to my children."

The Prophet then said:

"How good (are) the Quraishite women! (They are) ideal in observing their husbands' rights over them, and the most protectively sympathetic to their children!"

The Imam: A Peace Maker:

During his stay in Makkah, the Prophet, peace and blessings be upon him, sent contingents to quell some uprisings in the desert. They included a mission to Banu (tribe of) Jadhimah, which was headed by Khalid Ibn Al-Walid, a great military strategist. Although the people surrendered, Khalid had their members tied up, and then killed some of them. The Prophet, on hearing of that was very upset, as he sent these missions mainly to convey the call of Islam, not to fight unnecessarily. The Prophet was overheard praying:

"O Allah! You know that I disassociate myself from that action committed by Khalid!"

The Prophet then sent Imam Ali to repair that damage. Imam Ali paid blood compensations to the relatives of the victims. After everyone was satisfied, the Imam paid the balance which remained with him to them in order to make sure that they had no more claim to make from the Prophet. The Prophet was pleased with Imam Ali's action and endorsed it.

The Madinese Ansar group, while they were still in Makkah after its conquest, feared that the Prophet might decide to transfer his residence to Makkah. On hearing of that, he told them:

"O Ansar! To your town belong life and death."

Standing Firm at the Critically Grave Moment on the Day of Hunain:

On hearing of the surrender of Makkah to Islam, the neighboring desert tribes called Hawazin, in collaboration with the inhabitants of the town called *Al-Ta'if*, organized a huge army to attack and destroy the Prophet and his men. The Prophet, peace and blessings be upon him, after a fifteen-day stay in Makkah, moved out with his men on the way to a place called Hunain to meet those aggressors. The Muslim forces appeared to be a huge army, consisting of ten thousand men who came with the Prophet from Al-Madinah to Makkah, in addition to a few hundred more from Makkah. Some Muslims who were impressed with this size of the Muslim army remarked...unreasonably: "We cannot now be defeated on account of our number." Yet, while the Muslim army was passing through a low valley, unaware of the hiding Hawazin archers lurking at the higher edges of that valley, they became easy victims under the mercy of their enemies who rained them with their arrows suddenly shot at them. People ran away for their life, and there was a great confusion. Only a few remained firmly around the Prophet, including Imam Ali, Abu Bakr, Umar, Al-Abbas who was holding the tether of the Prophet's white mule, Al-Fadl Ibn Al-Abbas, Abu Sufyan Ibn Al-Harith, Rabi`ah Ibn Al-Harith, Usamah Ibn Zaid, and Ayman Ibn Umm Ayman who was soon killed in battle!

The Prophet, peace and blessings be upon him, called:

"O you people! Where (are you)? Come to me. Here I am. I am the Messenger of Allah, truly. I am Muhammad Ibn Abd Allah."

Al-Abbas, who had a powerful loud voice, repeated the call of the Prophet, and the Muslims rushed back to the Prophet, shouting:

"Here we are. Here we are!"

Once there were about one hundred of them, they fought harder and harder and, with the grace of Allah, the tables turned against the unbelievers and the victorious Muslims won, not only a great victory, but also enormous spoils of war..., men, women, and wealth. The Hawazin had come out en masse with their women, children, animals and belongings, thinking that this would spur their men to fight harder!

The Hawazin's flag carrier was very vociferous. Riding a red camel and holding his black flag attached to the top of his spear, he kept running enthusiastically, piercing his spear in the body of whoever he encountered from amongst the Muslims. Imam Ali severed the legs of the camel he was riding, causing him to fall on the ground, and he was then stabbed to death.

The Prophet then laid a siege against the people of Al-Ta'if, but when the siege was prolonged the siege was lifted! (The tribe of *Thaqif* later embraced Islam peacefully.)

In distributing the spoils taken from Hawazin, those who had recently embraced Islam from amongst the prominent leaders of Makkah were favored in order to soften their heart to Islam, like Abu Sufyan, Safwan Ibn Umayyah, and Mu`awiyah Ibn Abi Sufyan. Each one was given one hundred camels. Some got fifty, and some got less.

The Prophet Returns to Al-Madinah:

Before returning to Al-Madinah, the Prophet, peace and blessings be upon him, stopped at Makkah during the month of Zu Al-Qi`dah, the eleventh in the Hijrah year. He appointed Attab Ibn Asid as governor of Makkah at a salary of one *dirham* a day.

Tabuk Expedition:

The most major expedition undertaken by the Prophet after the conquest of Makkah was to *Tabuk,* a one-month journey from Al-Madinah. Having heard of the rise of the Muslim power in Arabia, the Byzantine authorities who were having under their control the Middle East coastal territories, started planning a hostile action against the young Islamic state. In fact, the Prophet, peace and blessings be upon him, had sent a message to Herecluse inviting him to embrace Islam, but there was no positive response.

In the circumstances, the Prophet organized his forces and presided over that expedition himself. As the Muslim army was to proceed at the peak of the summer heat, the Prophet left his entire family in Al-Madinah and asked Imam Ali Ibn Abi Talib to remain behind to take care of the family, which then included small young children.

The Muslim army, under the command of the Prophet, proceeded on its way to Tabuk during the month of Rajab, the seventh month of the Hijrah year. After their departure, some members of the Hypocrite group started talking about the Imam and the reason of his being left behind in the capital city of the state. They claimed that he was left behind because the Prophet did not have esteem for him. On hearing of this rumor, Imam Ali put on his armor and rushed to the Prophet, and he was able to reach him at a place called Al-Jurf, about three miles away from Al-Madinah. When the Prophet, peace and blessings be upon him, heard the story from the Imam, he said:

> "No! They are liars. I asked you to stay behind to take care of the family which is mine and yours. Would you not be satisfied that you are in relation to me in the same status as that of Harun (Aaron) to his brother Musa (Moses), except that no prophet shall be raised after me?"

The Imam returned to Al-Madinah reassured, and the Prophet, peace and pressings be upon him, continued his journey.

It seems that the Prophet, peace and blessings be upon him, also anticipated that there would be no serious engagement with the enemies who appear to have been frightened and avoided getting involved with the highly motivated Muslims at the time. And thus the need for the Imam at home was greater, and his stay in Al-Madinah at that particular time was amply justified.

Presiding over the Prophet's Funeral Service:

One of the important tasks performed by Imam Ali was his presiding over the team of men who undertook the funeral service on the noble body of the Prophet when he died on Monday,

Rabi` I, 11 A.H., (8 June 632 A.D.) The Prophet himself had recommended that members of his family should undertake those requirements. So it was Imam Ali who undertook the washing of the blessed body, assisted by Al-Abbas (his uncle), Al-Fadl Ibn Al-Abbas, Qutham Ibn Al-Abbas, Usamah Ibn Zaid, and Shuqran, (a former slave freed by the Prophet). Aws Ibn Khawliyy, a Khazrajite Madinese, was also admitted to take part by the Imam on his request in view of their relationship to the Prophet, through Abd Al-Muttalib's mother who was from them.

The washing was done on Tuesday. As it was customary before washing a dead person to take off the garment in which he had died, they debated the question as to whether or not to take off the Prophet's garment. Then they heard a voice ordering that his garment should be left on. Imam Ali rested the noble body on his bosom, Usamah and Shuqran poured water, Ali rubbed gently over the garment, and Al-Abbas, Al-Fadl and Qutham helped in turning it. When the washing was over, the noble body was shrouded in three garments. Throughout these processes, nothing but good odor emanated from the noble remains!

According to Abu Bakr, the Messenger of Allah had said that Prophets were buried where they died. Therefore, a grave was dug exactly under the place where the Prophet passed away. And when washing and shrouding were completed, the noble body was laid to rest at the edge of the grave, in accordance with the recommendation of the Prophet himself, peace and blessings be upon him. He was then left alone for a while, as the angels were supposed to come then and pray over him. Then men were allowed to go in groups to pray, but each by himself, not behind an imam. Then women were allowed to go and do likewise. Then youngsters were permitted to take their turn.

In the middle of the night on Wednesday, the noble body of the Prophet was laid to rest in his grave, by the team headed by Imam Ali. Five persons descended into the grave to undertake the careful method of laying the noble body to rest; namely, Imam Ali, Al-Fadl Ibn Al-Abbas, Qutham Ibn Abbas, Shuqran, and Aws Ibn Khawliyy. Sayyidah A'ishah said, "We became aware of the burying of the Prophet when we heard the sound of the dust being moved to fill up and cover the grave, in the middle of the night on Wednesday."

May peace and all the blessings be upon you, O Messenger of Allah!

Chapter VI

Merits of the Imam as Conveyed in Al-Qur'an and Al-Hadith

Readers will by now have learned a great deal of the virtues and the noble qualities of Imam Ali Ibn Abi Talib, may Allah be pleased with him and may He raise his status higher and higher with Him. However, let us quote here some of the relevant Qur'anic and Al-Hadith texts:

From the Holy Qur'an:

> "Do you consider providing water for pilgrims to drink and the maintenance of the Sacred Mosque equal to (the pious service of) those who believe in Allah and the Last Day, and strive with might in the cause of Allah? Surely Allah guides not the wrong-doers. Those who believed and emigrated leaving their homes, and strived hard, spent their wealth and laid their life for the cause of Allah, have the highest rank in the sight of Allah, and are the people who shall attain salvation. Their Lord gives them glad tidings of a mercy from Himself and of His good pleasure, and of Gardens for them, in which there are for them enduring delights, they shall dwell therein for ever! Surely Allah stores with Him great rewards." (Chapter ix, 19-22)

(It is related that this Qur'anic passage was revealed in the context of a situation in which some people vied in front of the Imam of their honorable function as custodians of the Allah's House, and some took pride in being in charge of providing water to pilgrims. The passage came down to assert the greater merit of the Imam's struggle in defending and promoting the cause of Allah.)

> "Your real friends are (no less than) Allah, His Messenger, and those who have believed,.... those who regularly observe the daily prayers and regularly pay charity,...(even) while they are bowing (in worship)." (v, 58)

The occasion on which this verse was revealed was as follows: One day, the Prophet was sitting in the mosque surrounded by some of his Companions. A beggar came and asked for charity. No one present had anything to offer. Imam Ali, who was praying and in the bowing position, shook a finger on which he was wearing a ring. The beggar jumped up, pulled the ring off and went away! The Prophet, who was impressed by the Imam's charitable spirit, raised his hands towards Heaven, and prayed:

> "O Allah. My brother Musa (Moses) prayed to You, saying: `O my Lord. Expand my breast, ease my task for me, and remove the impediment from my tongue so that they may understand me. And make for me a minister from my family, Aaron my brother. Add to my strength through him and make him share my task.' And then You, my Lord, revealed to him Your words: `Surely We shall strengthen your arm through your brother and invest you both with authority so that they cannot touch you.' And here I am, my Lord, Muhammad, Your Servant, Your Messenger and Your choice, O Allah, pleading to You! Expand my breast. Ease my burden for me. And make a member of my family, Ali, a minister for me. Add to my strength through him!"

Whereupon Gabriel came down from Heaven and revealed the Qur'anic words quoted above.

> "Those who spend in charity their wealth, by night and by day, in secret and in public, ... they shall have their rewards from Allah, and they shall suffer no fear or grief." (ii, 274)

It is said that the occasion on which this Qur'anic verse was revealed was the story when Imam Ali worked and earned four *dirhams*. Although he then had nothing else he gave away one *dirham* to a poor person he encountered while he was alone at night, and another *dirham* to another beggar he met when he had company during the same night. The following day, during the day-light time, he gave a *dirham* to a beggar he met in private and the last dirham to a needy person.

"Verily those who have believed and did righteous deeds,—they are the best of all creations." (xcviii:7)

It is related on the authority of Ibn Abbas that when that verse was revealed, the Prophet, peace and blessings be upon him, told Imam Ali:

"You and your supporters shall be raised on the Day of Judgment with the signs of satisfaction shining on your faces; whereas your adversaries shall come with gloomy countenances."

When verse 12 of chapter lxix was revealed, which reads:

"So that We may make it a reminder for you and that catching ears may retain its memory,"

the Prophet, peace and blessings be upon him, told Imam Ali:

"I prayed to Almighty Allah to make it your ears, O Ali!"

The Imam said:

"Ever since, I have never heard a speech from the Messenger of Allah except that I retained it and never forgot it."

When the Qur'anic verse, (chapter xiii, 7) was revealed, reading:

"And the unbelievers say, 'Why is not a sign sent down to him from his Lord,' but you are only a *warner*, and to every people there is a guide," the Prophet, peace and blessings be upon him, said to Imam Ali: 'I am the *warner* and Ali is the guide whereby those destined for salvation are rightly guided."

The Holy Qur'an, chapter lxxvi, verses 5-22 reads:

"The righteous will surely drink from a cup (the contents of which are) mixed with camphor, a fountain where the servants of Allah shall drink, making it flow in unstinted abundance. They fulfill (their) vows, and they fear a day the evil of which flies far and wide. And they feed, because of their love of Allah, the poor, the orphan and the captive, (saying): 'We feed you only for the sake of Allah, anticipating no reward or a word of thanks from you. We only fear from the side of our Lord a day of distressful wrath. (As a result of their righteous deed), Allah shall protect them from the hardship of that day, and shall shed over them a light of beauty and a (blissful) joy. And on account of their patience and forbearance, He shall reward them with a garden and (garments) of silk, reclining in it (the garden), on raised thrones, seeing (suffering) there neither the sun's (heat), nor excessive cold. And the shade of the (garden) will come low over them, and the bunches of fruit of it will hang low over them humbly. And round vessels of silver as well as goblets of crystal will be passed around for them, crystal clear, made of silver (which) they will measure (according to their wishes). And there, they will be given to drink of a cup mixed with *zanjabil*, a Fountain there called Al-Salsabil. And round about them there will be youth serving them, (who are) of perpetual freshness. If you see them, you would think they are scattered pearls. And if you should look there, you will see a bliss and a magnificent realm. Upon them (wearing) will be green garments of fine silk and heavy brocade, and they will be adorned with bracelets of silver; and their Lord will give them to drink a pure (delightful) drink. (And it will be said to them): This (is given to you as) a reward (for your endeavor) and your endeavor has been accepted and well recognized."

It is believed that the above Qur'anic passage was revealed in the context of the following story:

It is related that Al-Sayyidah Fatimah, the Prophet's daughter and the wife of the Imam, was given some wool to spin for a Jew in the neighborhood. From the wage she received for her service, an amount of barley was purchased. She pounded it and baked it. When the family gathered around the modest table to eat, someone appeared in front of the door and said:

"O members of the household of the Prophet, peace and blessings be upon him. I am a poor person, starving, and have nothing to eat."

Imam Ali and Al-Sayyidah Fatimah agreed to give him the bread she had baked, and the Imam, his wife and two children, Al-Hasan and Al-Husain, spent the night with empty stomachs!

The following day, Al-Sayyidah Fatimah did the same thing, and when the family gathered around the table, before any of them could have a bite, they heard someone at the door who said that he was a hungry orphan. They sent him their meal, and again the noble family had to go to bed with empty stomachs. On the third day, Al-Sayyidah Fatimah again prepared the meal, but when the family was about to start eating someone else appeared in front of the door and said that he was a hungry captive and pleaded for something to eat. The bread was handed over to him in the most noble degree of generosity and sacrificing! And so the above-quoted passage was revealed to celebrate that action.

The above Qur'anic quotations are probably enough; otherwise, it is said that there are three hundred Qur'anic verses alluding to the merits of Imam Ali Ibn Abi Talib. So, let us now move to quote some of the relevant hadiths speaking of the Imam's merits.

Prophetic Hadiths Concerning the Imam:

One day while the Prophet, peace and blessings be upon him, was resting in the mosque in the company of some of his Companions, including Imam Ali Ibn Abi Talib, two disputing parties came in and requested the Prophet to judge between them. The cow belonging to one of them had killed the donkey which belonged to the other. The owner of the cow was not willing to compensate the owner of the donkey for his loss.

Someone of those present rushed and said, "Animals cannot be held responsible for their deeds." Yet, the Prophet who did not seem to have been pleased with this hasty ruling, (and probably he also intended to reveal to the public the wisdom of Imam Ali), told the Imam: "O Ali! Settle this case!"

Imam Ali asked the disputing parties:

"Were the donkey and the cow both tied, or untied, or one of them tied and the other free? "

"The donkey was tied, but the cow was not tied, and her owner was around," came the answer.

"In that case, the owner of the cow has to pay compensation to the owner of the donkey," Imam Ali decided, and the Prophet, peace and blessings be upon him, endorsed the Imam's ruling and added:

"Aqdakum Aliyy," which means: "Ali is the best judge among you!"

Let us quote some more hadiths on the subject:
- "Whoever insults Ali is insulting me."

- "Whoever hurts Ali is hurting me."

- "Ali is part of me, and I am a part of him. Only Ali can act on my behalf."

- "Whoever loves Ali loves me."

- "Ali is the *imam* of the righteous, slayer of the wicked. Success is the reward for those who support him, and those who oppose him will be doomed to failure."

- "Ali is bound with the Qur'an, and the Qur'an is holding up to Ali. They never part company."

- "Ali will be a shining star in Paradise, like a planet shining to the earth's inhabitants."

- "Verily Paradise longs to welcome three persons: Ali, `Ammar and Salman! (That is `Ammar Ibn Yasir who, like his parents, suffered inhuman tortures at the hands of the polytheists of Makkah, and Salman the Persian who was an early convert to Islam)."

- "I am a *mawla* (a committed friend) of Ali. And any one who takes me as his *mawla*, Ali becomes his *mawla* as well."

This is a renowned hadith which was uttered by the Prophet, may peace and blessings be upon him, when he halted during one of his journeys by a water place known as *Ghadir al-Khumm*. It is related that the Prophet, peace be upon him, then called upon the people, and when they gathered, he declared that announcement, holding Imam Ali by hand.

- The Prophet also said:

"If I were the city of knowledge, Ali is its gate. So, whoever wishes to secure knowledge let him approach it through its gate."

- "The most knowledgeable person among my nation after me is Ali Ibn Abi Talib."

- When the Prophet, peace and blessings be upon him, decided to give his daughter, Fatimah, in marriage to Imam Ali, he told her:

"I am going to give you in marriage to a man who is the most knowledgeable of all people, and the most clement, and the earliest to embrace Islam."

- And the Prophet once told him

"O Ali! Among the believers, you were the first Muslim. Among the Muslims, you were the first Mu'min; and you are to me like what Harun (Aaron) was to Musa (Moses)."

-The Prophet also compared Imam Ali to Adam in his knowledge, to Nuh (Noah) in his understanding, to Ibrahim (Abraham) in his clemency, and to Yahya Ibn Zakariyya (John) in his vigor.

-The Prophet also said:

"People are created from different trees; but I and Ali belong to the same tree."

- And: "Looking at the face of Ali is a sort of worship."

- Imam Ali relates that the Prophet, peace and blessings be upon him, "called me once and told me:

"O Ali! You have a resemblance to Isa (Jesus) who the Jews hated so much that they made false accusations against his mother, and the Christians loved him so much that they raised him above his true status."

Imam Ali then added:

"Two categories of people go astray in attributing to me things from which I am free: those who exaggerate my status beyond my limitations and those whose hatred to me causes them to demean me!"

- When the Prophet's burial was completed, Imam Ali stood beside the noble grave and addressed the Prophet in the following words: "Fortitude is gracious except on your death; anxiety is vicious except over your departure, and the calamity of your absence from us is the greatest of all times!"

Chapter VII

11 - 35 AH (632-656 AD)

Status of the Imam During This Era, and Rise of the Question of the Caliphate:

Throughout this period, which is almost one quarter of a century, the Imam was out of the power center, and he led a life of an ordinary citizen though a prominent Companion of the Prophet, peace and blessings be upon him. He was respected for his wisdom, his knowledge, and for his close relationship to the Prophet. This era which followed the death of the Prophet, peace and blessings be upon him, started with a power struggle over the question as to who should step into the shoes of the Prophet, so to speak, to fill the vacuum created by the Prophet's death.

Of course no one could inherit the status of the Prophet as the recipient of the heavenly revelations. Muhammad Ibn Abd Allah was definitely the last in the line, the seal of the Prophets, as the Holy Qur'an categorically states. Religion had been completely revealed to Prophet Muhammad, who had delivered it fully to his contemporaries.

Function of the Caliph:

Besides receiving and conveying the heavenly revelations which ceased on his death, the Prophet, peace and blessings be upon him, exercised temporal power. He was like the head of state. He was responsible for the welfare, the security and the defense of the *ummah*, and for the administration of the state. He appointed governors of the provinces, collected the zakat taxes, promoted the well-being of the citizens, and settled their disputes. Therefore, as soon as he died, the need was felt for the installation of a successor to undertake these temporal burdens. Who, then, should be installed to shoulder these responsibilities?

The Imam's High Qualifications:

The eyes were focussed on a number of the Prophet's Companions, including, of course, Imam Ali Ibn Abi Talib who, in the eyes of his supporters and most probably in his own eyes, was the most qualified person for that high post on the following grounds:

- Imam Ali was a full cousin of the Prophet. The Prophet's father, Abd Allah, and Ali's father, Abu Talib, were full brothers. Their mother was Fatimah Binti `Amr, from the Makhzum tribe.

- Imam Ali was brought up under the care of the Prophet since he was a child. He was therefore like the Prophet's son. This was indeed a factor in widening the Imam's knowledge and in deepening his piety.

- Imam Ali was also the husband of Al-Sayyidah Fatimah, daughter of the Prophet and the closest person to his heart. He was also the father of Al-Hasan and Al-Husain, grandchildren of the Prophet who loved them very deeply and who described them as the masters of the youths in Paradise!

- More importantly, Imam Ali's daring performances and fearless courage in fighting the enemies of Islam was superb. He willingly and without hesitation laid down his life for the protection of Islam. He was one of the very few who remained with the Prophet at the two most critical moments on the Day of Uhud and the Day of Hunain, when almost every one else ran for his life! With a few others, he surrounded the Prophet to shield him from the arrows shot at him by the enemies, and then helped in washing and treating the Prophet's wounds, assisted by his wife Fatimah, caring less for the wounds he himself had sustained! His sacrifices and his successes elevated his status with Allah and with His Messenger!

- Imam Ali was universally acknowledged as the most eloquent and the most knowledgeable person among all the Prophet's Companions.

Factors Causing Delay in the Imam's Election to the Post of the Caliphate:

In spite of all these qualities and sacrifices, the chance for the Imam to succeed the Prophet and become the first caliph escaped from him, as did the chance to become the second or even the third! Let us see how all this happened.

In accordance with the recommendation of the Prophet himself, his own family should take care of his funeral procedure. Imam Ali, therefore, had to remain at the home of the Prophet, peace and blessings be upon him, to participate and oversee that procedure from the moment of the Prophet's death on Monday, 12th Rabi` I, 11 AH, till the burial of the noble body in the middle of the Wednesday night the fourteenth. By then, the first Caliph had been elected.

They first discussed the site of the Prophet's burial, whether it should be in his mosque or elsewhere. Abu Bakr then related that he had heard the Prophet say, "Prophets are buried where they die." So the noble body was moved and a grave was dug underneath the place where he was resting and died. Then they thought of removing the Prophet's garment in preparation for washing. Imam Ali (and Aishah too) related that they heard a voice commanding that his garment not to be removed. So the Prophet, peace and blessings be upon him, was washed with his garment on, and water was poured in a way that made it run underneath. Imam Ali held the noble body and let it rest on his chest, while water was poured by Usamah Ibn Zaid and Shuqran, a former slave freed by the Prophet, peace and blessings be upon him. The funeral team included Al-Abbas (the Prophet's uncle), his two sons Al-Fadl and Qutham, as well as Aws Ibn

Khawliyy, who represented the clan to which the grandmother of the Prophet's father belonged. Imam Ali also related: "The Messenger of Allah asked me to be the one responsible for washing him." Imam Ali never looked at the private parts of a human being, not even his own! Each member of the team, however, had his eyes covered with a piece of cloth tied around his head. The Prophet, peace and blessings be upon him, is related to have said,

"Anyone who attempts to look at my private parts shall have his eyes effaced!"

While Imam Ali was so engaged in those tasks, some leading members of the *Ansar* (the Madinese Supporters of the Prophet), raised the question of succession. Surely the mission of the Prophet in conveying the heavenly revelations had been fully completed before his death. But in addition to this unique superior task, the Prophet managed the worldly affairs of the nation in accordance with the divine guidance. So a group of the Ansar, led by Sa`d Ibn Ubadah gathered in the shade of a thatch called Thaqifat Bani Sa`idah, in Al-Madinah, as soon as they heard of the Prophet's death, and began to speak of the right of the Ansar to hold that office. Apparently Sa`d Ibn Ubadah's ambition was to hold that office. Umar Ibn Al-Khattab got a word about this development, and he alerted Abu Bakr who, along with Umar, went and joined the discussion. Abu Bakr persuaded the gathering that the Arabs would only submit to a Quraishite ruler, and Abu Bakr was chosen in that meeting to be the first caliph. Abu Bakr then moved to the Prophet's Mosque and received pledges of allegiance publicly. He then ascended the Prophet's pulpit and delivered his first speech, which may be described as his "inaugural address." It ran as follows:

"O people! I have been made to rule over you although I do not feel to be the best among you. If I do well support me, and if I go wrong resist me. Follow me as long as I am executing the commandments of Allah. Should I fail to do so, I shall have no right to claim your obedience. I say all this seeking Allah's forgiveness for myself and on your behalf."

Never has there been such an eloquent inaugural address, so effective, so meaningful and yet so short!

The Imam's Reaction to the Election of Abu Bakr:

Imam Ali raised no objection and voiced no protest against the election of Abu Bakr in order not to cause a division or a misunderstanding among Muslims. Only in respect of his wife's feeling, Al-Sayyidah Fatimah, the Prophet's daughter who was stricken with grief over her father's death and was somewhat displeased because of Abu Bakr's refusal to pay her inheritance from whatever wealth the Prophet had left behind, Imam Ali delayed announcing his pledge to Abu Bakr until shortly after her death, about six months after her father's death. Abu Bakr related that he had heard the Prophet say:

"We, the Prophets, are not to be inherited. Whatever we leave behind goes to charity."

Moreover, a person who succeeds a popular person is usually resented, no matter how innocent and how good the successor might be. That is why when the Prophet was still in his sick bed and he heard the voice of Umar leading the congregation in prayers at the mosque, not Abu Bakr to whom the Prophet had sent a message asking him to lead the congregational prayers in the mosque on his behalf, he blamed A'ishah, saying:

"You are indeed Yusuf's friends!"

The Prophet was alluding to the ladies who were so fascinated by Sayyidina Yusuf's charms that they cut their own fingers with the knives with which they were to cut the fruits offered to them by their host! That meant that A'ishah had probably failed to send the message to Abu Bakr, her father, so he would not be resented for standing on behalf of the Prophet during his illness.

After the death of Al-Sayyidah Fatimah, Imam Ali made an appointment to meet with Abu Bakr in the Prophet's mosque, bringing the Hashimite family with him. When all were gathered, Imam Ali stood up and said:

> "O Abu Bakr! We have been delayed in declaring our allegiance to you, not on account of denying your merits, or because of jealousy over something good Allah has favored you with; but we believe that we have a right in that matter that you have taken....."

Imam Ali is also related to have said:

> "You push the family of Muhammad away from his position and the status they should enjoy among people, and deny them their right. By Almighty Allah, we have a greater right in this matter than you do as long as there is among us some who can recite the Holy Qur'an..., who is established in legal matters....., who knows well the *Sunnah* of the Messenger of Allah..., who can undertake the responsibilities of the affairs of the people..., and can deal with them justly."

Abu Bakr also said a few good words praising the Hashimite family, and Imam Ali declared his allegiance to Abu Bakr publicly.

Caliph Abu Bakr Sought the Imam's Advice:

Abu Bakr respected Imam Ali very highly and consulted with him over major issues. Let us quote here the following relevant story. When Abu Bakr was considering the issue of sending troops to Syria to combat the Roman forces who were then in control of the Middle Eastern territories including Syria and Egypt and who had been provoking the newly young Muslim state at its borders, Abu Bakr invited the senior Companions, including Imam Ali, for consultation. Those present included Umar, Uthman Ibn Affan, Talhah Ibn Abd Allah, Al-Zubair Ibn `Awwam, and Abu `Ubaidah `Amir Ibn Al-Jarrah, Sa`d Ibn Abi Waqqas, Abd Al-Rahman Ibn `Awf, and of course the Imam. They all spoke in favor of the plan except Imam Ali, who remained silent. Abu Bakr then called him, saying:

"What do you think, Aba Al-Hasan?"

Imam Ali replied:

"If you confront the enemies, whether or not with you personally at the head in command, Allah shall grant you victory."

Very pleased with this assurance, Abu Bakr said to him:

"May Allah please you with good tidings. Please tell me how did you come to this conclusion?"

Imam Ali said:

"I heard the Messenger of Allah, may peace and blessings be upon him, say: `This religion (Islam) shall triumph over those who may dare to challenge it until it can stand on its own feet, and its adherents shall become masters of the world.'"

Abu Bakr said:

"How reassuring this hadith is! You have filled my heart with joy. May Almighty Allah bless you!"

Caliph Abu Bakr Invites the Imam to Address the Troops Going to Syria:

When the armies were organized, Imam Ali was invited to address them. He said:

"Praise be to Allah. Whatever he wishes will be, and whatever He does not wish cannot be! Had He wished, no two people could have differed, nor could the *ummah* have disputed over anything He had willed, nor would the less fortunate have still appreciated His favors. Destiny has gathered us here. Our Lord is hearing us and is seeing us. If He wishes we could be visited with a speedy calamity and our fortune could have been reversed! ... But Allah has made this world an abode of endeavor and of testing, and made the Hereafter the lasting abode (in order to punish the wrong-doers for their misdeeds and reward the good-doers for their good deeds.)

"You will soon be meeting those people (the enemies). So celebrate the night with prayers and the recitation of the Holy Qur'an, and plead to Almighty Allah for victory and forbearance. When you confront those people (the enemy), do so with determination and patience, and be true to your cause!"

Abu Bakr's Tremendous Services:

Abu Bakr died on 23 Jumada II, 13 AH. His caliphate, which lasted a little more than two years, was short but very effective. In spite of his physical fragility, Abu Bakr was a man of unshakable determination. As soon as the Arab bedouins in the various parts of Arabia heard of the Prophet's death, they reneged. Many apostatized, some claimed prophethood, and many others declared disobedience to the Madinan authority on the pretext that they were only committed to the Prophet personally. Against the advice of those around him who gave in to despair, Abu Bakr vowed to fight the apostates at all costs. Within six months he was able to re-unite the whole of Arabia under the Islamic flag, and then began the process of conquests outside Arabia.

Abu Bakr Appoints Umar as His Successor:

While he was on his death bed, Abu Bakr declared his decision to appoint Umar Ibn Al-Khattab as his successor, after consultation with most of the senior Companions, and he signed a document accordingly. He handed the Qur'anic pieces written at the time of the Prophet, to Umar for safekeeping. Thus the chance for Imam Ali even to succeed Abu Bakr was missed. Again Imam Ali did not object. He even gave his daughter Umm Kulthum in marriage to Umar, who respected the Imam and consulted the Imam over important matters. When Umar travelled, he appointed Imam Ali to take care of the administration of Al-Madinah. It is also said that Imam Ali served as the judge of Al-Madinah during the caliphate of Umar, which continued until 26 Zu Al-Hijjah, 23 AH, when he died as a result of a treacherous stabbing with a poisoned dagger by a Persian unbeliever!

Uthman Ibn `Affan, the Third Caliph:

Umar did not nominate a person to succeed him! Instead, he advised that one should be selected from a list of six men, those who had survived from the ten men the Prophet used to specifically praise and said would dwell in Paradise: Ali Ibn Abi Talib, Uthman Ibn `Affan, Talhah Ibn Abd Allah, Al-Zubair Ibn Al-`Awwam, Sa`d Ibn Abi Waqqas, and Abd Al-Rahman Ibn `Awf.

Umar advised that his popular pious son, Abd Allah, should not be elected to the office of the Caliphate, though his advice might be sought. He said that it was enough for the Al-Khattab clan to carry the burden of the caliphate once.

When the team of those distinguished men had a meeting, Abd Al-Rahman Ibn `Awf announced his decision to withdraw his candidacy, but requested to be trusted by the other members of the team to make his choice on their behalf after undertaking private consultations with each one of them. That was agreed. A date was set for announcing his decision.

On the third day after Umar's death, people gathered in the mosque to learn of the verdict. Abd Al-Rahman Ibn `Awf, wearing a head-gear that had been given to him by the Prophet and holding an unsheathed sword in his right hand, mounted the pulpit of the Prophet, peace and blessings be upon him, and declared:

> "O people! I have been consulting with you (privately) and have found out that you wish either Ali or Uthman (for the post of the caliphate).

Abd Al-Rahman then called:

"Ali! Rise."

Imam Ali went and stood up near the pulpit. Abd Al-Rahman held his right hand and told him:

> "Are you ready to commit yourself (if you are chosen for the post of the caliphate) to abide by Allah's Book and the Sunnah of His Messenger, and to follow the example of Abu Bakr and Umar?"

"Well! I am ready to do so as best as I can," replied Imam Ali.

Abd Al-Rahman released Ali's hand, and cried:

"Uthman! Rise!"

Uthman rose and walked to the pulpit. Abd Al-Rahman held his right hand and said:

> "Will you commit yourself to follow Allah's Book, the Sunnah of His Messenger and the example of Abu Bakr and Umar?"

"I do," Uthman responded, upon which Abd Al-Rahman turned his face up and prayed:

> "O Allah! You are hearing me. I have now surrendered my burden and transferred it to Uthman."

Abd Al-Rahman then climbed up and sat on the step on which the Prophet used to stand when he delivered his sermons. Uthman sat on the lower step and people rushed to shake his hand, declaring their allegiance to him one after another.

How disappointing this development must have been to the Imam's supporters! In a split second, just because of the Imam's careful yet positive answer, he lost the chance for the third time and to a member of the Umayyad clan who had never forgotten the enmity between Umayyah, the founder of their clan, and Hashim the great-grandfather of the Prophet and the Imam!

Uthman's Grave Trust of the Umayyads:

Uthman himself was a very good man, righteous and very generous with his wealth. He was an early Muslim, though not earlier than Imam Ali or as early as he. He was married to two of the Prophet's daughters, Ruqayyah and Umm Kulthum, one after the other. When the latter died, the Prophet, peace and blessings be upon him, told him: "Should we have another (unmarried) daughter, we would have offered her in marriage to you!" Unfortunately, members of the Umayyad clan, whom he trusted and who are said to be worldly-motivated, took advantage of his good-heartedness and harmfully interfered with the administration, as will be explained later. Let us for a moment meet with Imam Ali again.

Imam Ali's Restraint:

Imam Ali did not make a protest that he was stepped over, or for having been denied what, in view of a large section of the world of Islam at the time, was his privilege, in spite of provocation and attempt by some quarters to seduce him to mount a campaign of opposition. Even much earlier, when Abu Bakr was installed as the first caliph, it is related that Abu Sufyan Ibn Harb Ibn Umayyah, who embraced Islam only on the day of the conquest of Makkah in the eighth year after the Hijrah, and who had led the army of the polytheists during the campaigns at Uhud and Al-Khandaq earlier, approached Imam Ali and told him:

"If you wish, I would fill (the streets of) Al-Madinah with fighting horses and troops, and block all entrances leading to it."

Imam Ali responded:

"No, Aba Hanzalah! You are attempting to conduce us to do something not in keeping with our manners or our morality. I have already closed all gates leading to such unbecoming actions and turned away (to the path of righteousness).

Blessings of the Imam's Neutrality during This Era:

The Imam's neutrality and his freedom from administrative engagement during that era was a blessing for his contemporaries and more so for us, the generations of Islam which followed the Imam's time. Even Abu Bakr and Umar benefited from his knowledge, for both sought and requested his verdicts. We may recall here the case of a woman who delivered a baby after a six-month pregnancy. Umar was about to apply the punishment to her, as if she had committed adultery. She was saved by Imam Ali, who gave a fatwa that pregnancy could be six months only on the grounds of the following Qur'anic verses:

"We have enjoined upon man kindness to his parents: In pain did his mother bear him, and in pain did she give him birth. The carrying of the child to his weaning is (a period of) thirty months." xlvi, 15

"And We have enjoined upon man (to be good) to his parents: in travail upon travail did his mother bear him, and his weaning is in two years." xxxl, 14*

We may also recall here the amusing story which occurred during Umar's caliphate, in which a man was accused of saying:

---

*So, two years of nursing taken away from 30 months, six months remain.

"I have risen this morning, feeling to be fond of *fitnah* (which apparently means `disturbances'), hating *Al-Haqq* (which means `the truth' and could even be a name of God)." The man added: "I also believe in the claims made by the Jews and the Christians, and believe in that which I cannot see and confess of that which is not created."

When the case was brought up to Caliph Umar, he requested the Imam's opinion before inflicting punishment upon that person. When the Imam arrived and Caliph Umar related to him the story, the Imam commented:

"The man is correct. He loves wealth and children, which are described in the Qur'anic verse lxiv, 15 as *fitnah*. He declared that he disliked *Al-Haqq*, which is a name of death as in the Qur'anic verse L, 21; and he agreed with the claim of the Jews in asserting that "The Christians have nothing to stand upon," and agreed with the claim made by the Christians that the Jews had nothing to stand upon, as quoted in the Holy Qur'an (ii,1130). He is right in believing in a Reality he does not see, namely, Allah, and confesses of something not yet created, which is the Day of Judgment."

When Caliph Umar consulted with the Prophet's Companions as to the need for fixing a point of time to be the start of the Islamic calendar, it was Imam Ali who proposed the date of the Hijrah.

Uthman, the third Caliph, was at first amenable to the Imam's advice. But when the Caliph later became dominated by members of the Umayyad clan, the Imam's presence was ignored, much to the misfortune of the ummah. Nevertheless, when the Imam heard that Caliph Uthman was besieged in his residence and surrounded by rebels demanding the surrender of Marwan Ibn Al-Hakam, he sent his illustrious sons Al-Hasan and Al-Husain to stand guards at the door of the caliph's residence to protect him from the hands of the rebels. And when he heard that the caliph was not allowed to have drinking water, the Imam sent him a water skin. It seems that no one anticipated that the rebels were after the person of the caliph himself or that the rebels would climb over the back wall into the caliph's chamber. That is why when the Imam heard of the tragedy which claimed the caliph's life, he rushed to the caliph's residence and blamed his own children and is even said to have beaten them!

These tragic developments ended the era during which the Imam devoted his time to worship, teaching, and giving advice when an advice was sought.

The Imam Was the Founder of the Branches of Islamic Knowledge:

So, the Imam's freedom from administrative and similar burdens during this era of his life was a great blessing to the world of knowledge. He had more time to impart his treasures to devoted disciples such as his younger cousin, Abd Allah Ibn Abbas. They both formed something like an informal academy, the first of its kind in Islam. Through it, the Imam's knowledge was transmitted to the succeeding generations, each generation transmitting it to the next succeeding generation. In this way, they bequeathed to us the Islamic academic heritage, including the fields of theology, law, ethics, and linguistics.

For example, in the field of theology, the leader of the Mu`tazilite group, Wasil Ibn `Ata' can trace the chain of his teachers to the Imam. He studied under Abd Allah Ibn Muhammad Ibn Al-Hanafiyyah, Ibn Al-Imam Ali, nicknamed Abu Hashim. This Abu Hashim studied under his father Muhammad who, in turn, studied under his father Imam Ali. In the same way, Imam Abu Al-Hasan Al-Ash`ari, the imam of the Sunni group, can trace the series of his teachers, since his major teacher was Abu Ali Al-Jubba'i who studied under Wasil Ibn `Ata'.

In the field of Islamic law, the founders of the legal schools also trace their academic descent to Imam Ali. As we know, Imam Abu Hanifah was a disciple of Imam Ja`far Al-Sadiq, who studied under his father Imam Muhammad Al-Baqir, who learned from his father Imam Ali Zain Al-Abidin, who studied under his father Imam Al-Husain and his uncle Al-Hasan, and those, Al-Hasan and Al-Husain, studied under the Imam. Imam Malik, who taught Imam Al-Shafi`i, studied under Rabi` at Al-Ra'y, who studied under `Ikrimah who, in turn, studied under Abd Allah Ibn Abbas, who was a disciple of Imam Ali.

These lineal series of teachers do not represent the full situation. Otherwise, in each generation there was a wide complex network of scholars, and each scholar learned from a number of teachers, often in different localities. Traveling near and far in search of knowledge was an established tradition, and nearly every one of those renowned scholars sustained a number of long journeys in search of knowledge. Fortunately for those scholars, the entire Muslim world was a home for each one of them. They often died in towns of countries far away from their place of birth. Imam Al-Shafi`i, for example, was born in Ghazzah, studied in Makkah and in Al-Madinah, travelled to Yemen, Iraq (twice), and died in Egypt at the age of 54 years. Imam Al-Humaidi of Andalusia died in Baghdad, and Abu Bakr Ibn Al-Arabi, also of Andalusia, died in Damascus. Imam Ali, the Great, our hero in this modest work, seems to have set the model for those great scholars. He was born in Makkah, flourished in Al-Madinah, and died in Al-Kufah, a town started under caliph Umar in Iraq!

Imam Ali's contribution to the field of moral and ethical studies is well recognized, as is his contribution to literary and grammatical studies. Imam Ali Ibn Abi Talib was the scholar who first conceived of the concept of "word" as the basic unit of speech and of its division into "nouns," "verbs," and "particles." Let us listen to the following story related by Abu Al-Aswad Al-Du'ali of Al-Basrah:

"I went once to visit the Imam and found him engaged in deep thinking, with his head slightly lowered. I inquired:

"What is it that is engaging you so much, O Commander of the Faithful?"

"I have heard people in this town of yours making grammatical errors in their speech, and I have thought of composing a book on the rules governing the Arabic language," the Imam replied.

"If you do so, you will revive us and perpetuate the language among us," I commented.

"After three days, he handed over to me a plate on which he had written:

"In the name of Allah, the Merciful, the Compassionate. A word is a noun, a verb, or a particle. A noun is a word which denotes a name (of a person, a thing, a thought, etc.); a verb denotes a movement, and a particle is a word that denotes a meaning which is neither a noun or a verb."

"And things are three (categories): a clear noun, a pronoun, and something that is neither of these (perhaps the demonstrative pronoun). Scholars are graded (or differed in) defining this category of words which are neither nouns nor pronouns."

"He then told me," Abu Al-Aswad added:
"Pursue this *nahw* (direction), O Aba Al-Aswad."

And as a result, this area of study came to be known as `*Ilm Al-Nahw*. The contribution of Imam Ali to starting and developing the study of the Islamic subjects was immensely very great. It is worthy of a separate independent investigation.

Chapter VIII

Imam Ali Ibn Talib: The Fourth Caliph

His Election to the Post of the Caliphate:

This was by far the toughest part of the life of the Imam during which he was put to the toughest test. His qualities of patience, perseverance, magnanimity, chivalry, propriety, and piety proved themselves to be true in the highest degree.

In the aftermath which followed the murder of the third caliph, Uthman Ibn Affan, the responsible inhabitants of Al-Madinah searched for the Imam to urge him to take up the post of the caliphate. Knowing their intention, the Imam, who had become disinclined to accepting that post in view of the humiliating end of the third caliph and feeling sick of the ill treatment meted out to Uthman, Imam Ali had gone into hiding in the orchards around the town. The rebels also searched for the Imam to plead to him to accept the post. They feared for their own safety if they should start on their way home while the post remained vacant.

When the Imam was found and offered the post of the caliphate, he declined and said, "I am to you as a minister better than a commander." After much pressure, the Imam yielded, fearing the consequences that might befall the ummah should the post have remained vacant for too long. He insisted, however, that allegiance to him should be pledged publicly in the mosque. This was duly done. Among the notable personalities who pledged their allegiance so early to the Imam were Talhah Ibn Abd Allah and Al-Zubair Ibn Al-`Awwam, two senior Companions of the Prophet, as well as all the Companions residing in Al-Madinah. This was accomplished on Friday 25 Zu Al-Hijjah 35 AH. (July 6, 655 AD.) Only very few Companions hesitated to pledge their allegiance to the Imam, either to give themselves more time to think about it or because of their Umayyad allegiance. One of these, called Al-Nu`man Ibn Bashir, carried the garment of Caliph Uthman in which he was murdered, stained with his blood, and ran out with it and gave it to Mu`awiyah Ibn Abi Sufyan, the governor of Syria who was related to Uthman.

The Imam's Inaugural Address:

When the Imam was selected as the fourth caliph, and he agreed to take up that post after much reluctance, he mounted the pulpit, expressed thanks and gratitude to Almighty Allah, and then said:

"Verily Almighty Allah has revealed a Book as a guidance. In it, He showed the distinction between good and evil. So follow that which is good and avoid that which is evil. Perform the religious obligations for the sake of Almighty Allah, and He will lead you on the way to Paradise."

"Verily Allah has forbidden things which are well known, and has raised the sanctity of the Muslim person over all other sanctities. And He has brought together the Muslims in a strong bond of sincerity and monotheism. A Muslim is he from whose hand and tongue Muslims are spared—except for some lawful factors. It is forbidden to cause hurt to a Muslim, unless there is some lawful action. Protect the rights due to the public. Death is lying in ambush. People came before you, and the Day of Resurrection is behind you. Make your burden light so that you can catch up. People are only awaiting their end. Fear Allah, O you, His servants in His servants and in His Land. You are to be brought to account for all that you may do (and in how you deal with His creations), even your treatment of the land and the animals. Obey

Almighty Allah, and disobey Him not. Whenever you see a chance to do good, grab it; and if you should sense some evil thing, keep away from it. `And recall when you were a small band despised in the land, and afraid that people might despoil and kidnap you; but Allah provided you with a safe asylum for you, and strengthened you with His aid, and gave you good things for sustenance that you might be grateful.'"

A Hopeful Aspiration:

When Imam Ali was so elected to the post of the caliphate, a general air of relief was felt, and everyone hoped that an era of peace and tranquility would prevail, during which the great Imam, with his talents and experiences, would successfully work for the greater glory of Islam and more happiness and prosperity for the people. Unfortunately, Imam Ali was denied that chance, and instead he had to struggle to put down unjustified rebellions and uprisings.

Relief of the Provincial Governors:

Imam Ali, a man of deep piety and sensitive conscience, strongly felt that it would be a religious compromise to allow those unscrupulous governors appointed during the time of `Uthman to remain in office one single day unnecessarily. He therefore lost no time before writing to each one of them, summoning them to come to see him in Al-Madinah. He did not listen to the advice honestly given him by sincere associates such as his younger cousin, Abd Allah Ibn Abbas who was of the view to let these governors stay for a while until he had received their allegiance and stabilized his own position, and he could then handle their cases more leisurely and effectively.

Mu`awiyah Disobeys:

Attention was focused upon the response of Mu`awiyah Ibn Abi Sufyan. Mu`awiyah embraced Islam on the day of the conquest of Makkah, in 8 A.H. Like his father, Abu Sufyan, Mu`awiyah was given one hundred camels of the spoils from the tribes of the Hawazin. The Hawazin declared war on the Prophet immediately after the conquest of Makkah. The Prophet, peace and blessings be upon him, met the Hawazin and defeated them at Hunain. These gifts were given to them, Mu`awiyah and his father, by the Prophet in order to soften the sharp edge of their opposition to Islam. Mu`awiyah became thereafter one of the scribes of the Prophet who also included Imam Ali himself. The Imam is credited to have written for the Prophet two of the most historical documents: The treaty concluded between the Prophet and the polytheists of Makkah on the Day of Al-Hudaibiyah referred to earlier, and the document known as *Al-Sahifah*, which was dictated by the Prophet shortly after his immigration to Al-Madinah. This latter was an important document which set out the terms of mutual responsibilities between the tribal groups inhabiting Al-Madinah at that time; namely, the Muslim immigrants, the Arab tribes of Al-Madinah, and the Jews. The document, which attracted attention in recent years and is often referred to as the Constitution of Al-Madinah, amounts to a declaration on the sanctification of the town of Yathrib which the Prophet re-named *Al-Madinah*, and it also set out the terms of settling disputes arising from crimes against human lives.

Confident of his strong position and popularity in Syria, Mu`awiyah delayed answering Caliph Ali for three months. During his long rule, first as the Governor of Damascus, a post in which he was appointed by Umar, and then as the Governor of the entire Syria, added to him by Uthman, Mu`awiyah did everything to capture the hearts of the Syrians to his side, occasionally using the treasury resources under his hand. The Syrians became very loyal to him and were prepared even to lay down their own lives for his personal glory. Mu`awiyah also struck up a friendship with `Amr Ibn Al-`As, an able military commander who was responsible for the conquest of Egypt under `Umar Ibn Al-Khattab, and a shrewd politician himself.

After a three-months's delay, Mu`awiyah sent a challenging reply to Imam Ali, the new caliph. He sent his own messenger with some verbal instructions and a folded sheet with no writing on it except the words: "From Mu`awiyah Ibn Abi Sufyan to Ali Ibn Abi Talib," and affixed his seal on it. Mu`awiyah advised his messenger to arrive in Al-Madinah during the daytime and to hold the folded sheet supposed to contain his answer to the caliph in front of his face to attract attention.

Mu`awiyah's messenger did as he was told. He arrived at Al-Madinah on 10 Rabi` I, 36 A.H. and attracted attention by the way he walked, marching towards the office of the caliph. People, eager to know what response Mu`awiyah sent to the caliph, followed him to the Imam's office. When the Imam found the sheet empty from any true message, he asked the messenger;

"What message do you have?"

"I have left behind, out there, a people who are determined not to accept lesser than revenge!", the messenger replied after receiving from the Caliph an assurance of a safe passage.

"Revenge from whom?," the caliph wondered.

"From the veins in Ali's neck," The messenger dared to say! And he added:

"And I left behind sixty thousand men crying under Uthman's garment hanging on the pulpit of the mosque (in Damascus), stained with his blood, and the chopped-off fingers of (Uthman's wife) Na'ilah, stuck to it!"

"What do they want?," the Caliph asked once again.

"Revenge for Uthman's blood", the messenger answered, upon which the caliph reflected:

"From me they want revenge for Uthman's blood! O Allah! You know I am innocent of having anything to do with Uthman's blood!"

Serious Cleavage by Three Senior Companions:

Meanwhile, Talhah and Al-Zubair reneged on their pledge. They went to Makkah and joined Al-Sayyidah A'ishah who had gone there originally for pilgrimage but, hearing of Uthman's murder, became very disturbed and called for the revenge of his blood, supported by Talhah and Al-Zubair. Then they all moved to Basrah to rally support for themselves and fought its governor, Uthman Ibn Hanif, Imam Ali's man. They defeated him and put him into prison after pulling out his hair and eyelashes!

Ummu Salamah Warns A'ishah:

When Al-Sayyidah A'ishah got herself deeply involved in the disturbances which followed the murder of the third caliph, Uthman Ibn Affan, Al-Sayyidah Ummu Salamah, another widow of the Prophet, wrote to Al-Sayyidah A'ishah urging her to keep away from the dispute and not to get much involved. Although the letter fell on a deaf ear, it is interesting to record it here:

After invoking the name of Allah and saying a prayer over the Prophet, peace and blessings be upon him, the letter says:

"Harken you! You are the link between the Messenger of Allah and his *ummah*, and your veil is spread over his honor. The noble Qur'an defended your honor, so keep it up. It gave you mental respite, so let it not be lost. Allah is behind this ummah, (He will take care of it). The Messenger of Allah was so close to you that if it were to be so, he would have appointed you. You know, the pillar of the religion, if it should bend, cannot be straightened by women, nor could it be repaired if it should split. Women's honor lies in lowering their gaze and lengthening the tail of their garment. What would you say to the Messenger of Allah, peace and blessings be upon him, if you imagine him encountering you on the top of a mountain or in the bottom of a valley riding on the back of a young camel, from a desert halting place to another desert halting place hoping that Allah might fill your ravine, then you counter the Messenger of Allah with his veil ravaged by you, the veil on which Allah had taken your pledge. If I myself should have attempted your adventure, and then I am told, `Go into Paradise,' I would be ashamed to meet with Allah, having violated the ceiling under which I was covered by Him. So, make the veil which was spread over you your citadel. Make it your home until the day you meet with Him. The best way to obey Allah is when you stick to your home, and the wisest is to make your activities within it. If I should attempt to remind you of all that which was said by the Prophet, peace and blessings be upon him, you would bite me like a serpent!"

However, this noble intervention on the part of Al-Sayyidah Ummu Salamah, was unfortunately not heeded!

The Imam Struggles to Clear the Misunderstanding: The Camel Battle (Near Al-Basrah):

Imam Ali, who was very keen to preserve Muslim blood at any cost, left Al-Madinah with two hundred men and went toward Al-Basrah. Halting at a place called *Dhu Qar*, the Imam sent letters to Al-Sayyidah A'ishah, Talhah, and Al-Zubair pleading to their consciences and reminding them of their merits and their early contributions in the service of Islam. This diplomatic method appeared to be successful, as all parties agreed to make peace and abandon the idea of resorting to hostilities. Imam Ali was very happy, and an atmosphere of peace and friendliness appeared to dominate.

Before the two forces dispersed, however, certain elements within the Imam's camp feared that the climate of peace might expose them and reveal their crimes which led to the murder of the third caliph. So in the middle of the night, they began hostilities against the camp of Al-Sayyidah A'ishah. Innocent people were drawn to fighting, each party thinking it was a treachery committed by the other. Soon an all-out war broke out, although Al-Zubair had withdrawn and left for the Hijaz. Talhah also decided to go, but was hit by an arrow shot by Marwan Ibn Al-Hakam and killed. The fighting between the two forces increased with the break of the daylight, and each party sustained heavy casualties. People rallied around the camel which Al-Sayyidah A'ishah was riding. The Imam ordered that enough men of his own should stay close to her camel to protect her from falling or molestation. In order to shorten the war, the Imam ordered the camel to be killed, while Muhammad Ibn Abu Bakr, her brother, was on the spot. He helped her out from her litter, and the hostilities stopped. She was then given a respectable temporary accommodation prior to her journey back to Al-Madinah.

When the war broke out, the Imam ordered that no fleeing warrior should be chased, no property should be taken away, and the privacy of the homes should not be violated.

This battle took place on Jumada II, 36 A.H. The Imam lost in this battle 1,070 of his 20,000 men, whereas the party of Al-Sayyidah A'ishah lost 15,720 out of a total of 30,000 men. When the war was over, the Imam paid a courtesy visit to Umm Al-Mu'minin Al-Sayyidah A'ishah and greeted her in the following words:

"Peace be upon you, Mother. May Almighty Allah forgive you."

"And may He forgive you too," she responded.

The victorious Imam, who earlier prayed the funeral prayer service over all the victims from his and from the other parties, then arranged for sending Al-Sayyidah A'ishah back home in a dignified manner, surrounded by a bodyguard of twenty persons whose heads were wrapped and who held swords in their hands. Al-Sayyidah A'ishah felt rather uneasy for being surrounded all the way by a party of men. But on arrival at her destination, those persons took off their turbans revealing their femininity.

Al-Sayyidah A'ishah must have appreciated that gracious treatment of the Imam. It may have even repaired the tension that had existed in their relationship since the time of the scandal fabricated against her by the hypocrites. It is related that while all other members of the household of the Prophet defended her, the Imam instead told the Prophet:

> "You may divorce her. There are many other women. You may also ask her slave girl. She will tell you the truth."

The slave girl stated in her testimony that there was nothing wrong whatsoever in the behavior of Umm Al-Mu'minin, except that she sometimes let sleep overtake her when she was asked to watch the dow, thus letting the birds ravish it. As we all know, however, the Holy Qur'an came down asserting the innocence of Al-Sayyidah A'ishah.

While the Imam was inspecting the victims of the war, he passed by the body of Talhah Ibn Abd Allah. With tears shed from his eyes, the Imam said:

> "It is unbearable for me, O father of Muhammad, to see you lying so exposed! I wish that I was dead twenty years before!"

As for Al-Zubair, he was unfortunately killed while he was engaged in prayers on his way back to Al-Madinah, at a place near present-day Kuwait. His murderer brought Al-Zubair's sword to Imam Ali, believing that the Imam would be glad to learn of the death of a challenger. Instead, the sad Imam related the hadith in which the Prophet said:

> "Give the murderer of Al-Zubair the tiding that he will be among the people of the Hellfire!"

The Battle of the Camel was the first bloody hostility among Muslims. There is no doubt that the heart of the Imam was deeply regretful that he had to fight his co-believers with the sword with which he had fought the polytheists at the time of the Prophet. He had, however, to defend the integrity of the state.

The Battle at Siffin:

As if the loss of so many precious Muslim lives and great energetic efforts wasted were not enough, Mu`awiyah challenged the Imam. With 120,000 fighters, he camped at a place called *Siffin*, near the Euphrates River in Iraq. That was early Zu Al-Hijjah, 36 A.H. Mu`awiyah and his men occupied the area dominating the source of drinking water. The Imam marched to meet Mu`awiyah with 90,000 of his supporters. Mu`awiyah and his men refused to grant access to drinking water to the Imam's army, despite repeated appeals from the Imam! A contingent from the Imam's forces was able to remove Mu`awiyah's men from the area dominating the drinking water, and the Imam refused to deny Mu`awiyah's army access to the drinking water!

Here again, the Imam did not wish to shed Muslim blood unnecessarily. He did his utmost to persuade Mu`awiyah to come to terms with him in the best interest of Islam, but these efforts were in vain! For example, on Saturday 1 Zu Al-Hijjah of the Hijrah year 36, the Imam sent a message to Mu`awiyah through Bashir Ibn `Amr Al-Ansari and Habib Ibn Rib'i:

> "O Mu`awiyah! This near (material) world is short lived, and you will be returning to the Hereafter in which Allah shall indeed bring you to account and inflict upon you the evil consequences of your deeds. In the name of Allah, I urge you not to split the ummah and not to shed its blood."

Mu`awiyah interrupted the messenger and said:

> "Why don't you go to your master and offer him your advice?"

Bashir said:

> "My master has no equal. He is an early believer and a close relative of the Allah's Messenger, peace and blessings be upon him."

"What do you want me to do?," Mu`awiyah retorted.

"To fear Allah and to listen to the call of your cousin to follow the truth. This will be better for you now and in the Hereafter."

Mu`awiyah retorted:

"You want me to abandon demanding revenge of Uthman's blood? Never!"

In the circumstances, the Imam had no alternative but to meet Mu`awiyah with 90,000 men, and he camped near Siffin. Mu`awiyah denied Ali's men access to drinking water, in spite of appeals sent to him by the Imam. On the Imam's order, Mu`awiyah's men were moved away from the passage to drinking water, but he graciously ordered that they should not be deprived of it!

That unfortunate battle, which was again forced on the Imam and which lasted one hundred and ten days, costing the Imam 25,000 precious lives against 35,000 Syrians, demonstrated the Imam's unique military talents, his prowess, his dignity and his nobility. As no one dared to challenge him, the Imam had to fight hiding his identity. Once his victims fell to the ground and realized who it was, they raised their legs, exposing their private endowments, thus forcing the magnanimous Imam to turn away from them!

When an all-out war broke out between the two parties, the Imam's party routed their enemies due to their able leadership. When a decisive victory was in sight, and Mu`awiyah's party was about to withdraw, they resorted instead to a cunning strategy advised by `Amr Ibn Al-`As. Knowing that among the Imam's men there was a group of foolish, fanatic and strongheaded people, they raised Qur'anic sheets on the points of spears, meaning to say: "Let us resort to the judgment of the Qur'an."

The Imam warned that this was a cunning stratagem that the other party resorted to in order to escape from defeat. But that stupid and strong-headed group forced the Imam to stop fighting by threatening to kill him and his generals who might have hesitated to stop fighting! And so a chance to gain a victory by the Imam that would have most probably led to the unification of the world of Islam and restoring it to its past glory and dignity was lost!

The rest of the whole story is disheartening. While the Imam remained faithful to his ideals of honesty, sincerity, and always true to his word, the other party resorted to expediency, manipulation, and even treachery. A process of tahkim (arbitration), was agreed to by both parties after hesitation on the part of the Imam, who was sure of the insincerity of the other party. It ended in a fiasco manipulated by `Amr Ibn Al-`As, who represented Mu`awiyah. The result was that Mu`awiyah earned greater prestige in the eyes of his Syrian supporters, while the virtuous Imam was left with a divided army, even though he had on his side several Companions who had been praised by the Prophet.

Arbitration and Consequences:

The post-Siffin era must have been very painful. It was painful to see the consequences of ending the war at Siffin just about when a decisive victory was in sight! Mu`awiyah gained greater popularity among the Syrians. He began to enlarge his kingdom and assumed the title *Amir Al-Mu'minin*, whereas the Imam's men were wavering. The Imam had lost during the war at Siffin such great eminent supporters as Ammar Ibn Yasir on whom the Imam could count. He lost Al-Ashtar, a great general and a faithful supporter of the Imam who died as a result of an intrigue said to have been manipulated by the Imam's enemies! Poison was mixed in his drink while he was on his way to Egypt!

And the result of the so-called *Arbitration* was as sad as the Imam had anticipated! He knew that Abu Musa Al-Ash`ari, a good-hearted man, was no match for `Amr Ibn Al-`As. He nominated Abd Allah Ibn Abbas or Al-Ashtar as an arbiter with `Amr who was quite a shrewd person. But he was not allowed to make his choice and was compelled to accept Abu Musa's nomination under threat!

When Abu Musa and `Amr met to deliberate as arbiters, `Amr persuaded Abu Musa that the best way out of the confusion caused by the dispute over the post of the caliphate was to declare rejection of the disputing parties and leave it to the ummah to make its own choice.

Throughout their private meetings, `Amr treated Abu Musa very respectfully, emphasizing the fact that Abu Musa was a much earlier convert to Islam and recalling the Prophet's praise of Abu Musa. The latter assumed that it was a sort of honest, sincere treatment in view of Abu Musa's seniority. Let us relate the scenario of what transpired on the day on which the recommendation of the arbiters was to be announced.

Imam Ali, may Allah be pleased with him, sent four hundred of his men, headed by his cousin Abd Allah Ibn `Abbas to the site of the declaration. Mu`awiyah sent an equal number. The town was Dawmat al Jandal. Some notable Muslims were also present, among them Abd Allah Ibn Umar, Abd Al-Rahman Ibn Abi Bakr, and Abd Al-Rahman Ibn Al-Zubair.

When all were there and every one was ready and eager to hear the verdict, Abu Musa and `Amr appeared and walked to the pulpit. `Amr insisted that Abu Musa should announce the verdict first, apparently out of respect. Abd Allah Ibn `Abbas then got up and called upon Abu Musa:

"O Abu Musa! If you have agreed with him (`Amr) on a solution, let him speak first."

Abu Musa responded, saying:

"We have already agreed, and there is not to be a dispute over our agreement."

Then Abu Musa delivered the following speech:

"O people! We have looked into the current situation of the *ummah*, and have agreed that there is no course of action better for the *ummah* than removing both Ali and Mu`awiyah from the candidacy for the post of the caliphate, and then leave it to the ummah to select another candidate. Accordingly, I declare the removal of both Ali and Mu`awiyah. So choose yourselves for the post whoever you believe to be the best in your views."

Abu Musa then moved aside, and `Amr took his place and said:

"Abu Musa has removed his master, as you have heard, and I too do remove him, but at the same time I support my friend Mu`awiyah and confirm him as the legitimate caliph. He is Uthman's heir and the man entitled to claim restitution for his blood and has the greatest right to replace him!"

Abu Musa then angrily shouted at him, saying:

"What happened to you? You are just like a dog. If you attack him he lolls out his tongue, or if you leave him alone he still lolls out his tongue!"

`Amr retorted:

"And you are like a donkey which carries huge tomes but understands them not!"

Abu Musa, deeply regretting having trusted `Amr, ran away to Makkah. The people became very confused, while Mu`awiyah took the best advantage of the confusion, henceforth posing as the legitimate caliph!

When Ibn Abbas and Al-Qadi Shuraih, who had been sent to lead the Imam's delegation, went to Al-Kufah and conveyed to the Imam what transpired as a result of the arbitration, the Imam mounted the pulpit and addressed his audience as follows:

"Praise be to Allah, even though time has brought about a crushing calamity and great misfortune. There is no

God but He. (And I bear witness that) Muhammad is His servant and His Messenger, peace and blessings be upon him.

"Harken, O people! Sin verily causes sorrow and leads to deep regret.

"I had given you my opinion about these two men and about this (so-called) arbitration. You insisted on following your own view and disregarded my opinion. So I and you resembled the regrettable situation lamented by the poet of the Hawazin tribe, who said:

`I offered them my opinion at *Mun'arij Al-Liwa*,
But they did not appreciate the value of my
advice until late morning the next day!'

"Those two men you chose as arbiters have thrown the ruling of the Qur'an behind their back. They revived what the Qur'an had caused to die, and each one of them followed his own whims and disregarded Allah's guidance. They ruled without clear evidence or known custom. They differed between themselves, and both have gone astray!"

Emboldened by the inconclusive result of the arbitration, Mu`awiyah began to send his forces to encroach upon the territories under the Imam. A contingent led by `Amr Ibn Al-aAs defeated Muhammad Ibn Abi Bakr, the Imam's ruler of Egypt, and `Amr took it over as Mu`awiyah's Governor of Egypt. And while Mu`awiyah's men were so active causing disturbances here and there, many of the Imam's men became unenthused and reluctant, much to the disappointment of the Imam, who vented his feelings in speeches and eloquent sermons, some of which are recorded in the collections of his addresses edited by Al-Sharif Al-Radi, and published under the title *Nahj Al-Balaghah*. Even Mu`awiyah began to send a representative to oversee Al-Hajj season, a privilege so far belonged to the caliph alone. It was Imam Ali alone who sent such a representative every year.

His representative in the year 38 AH was Qutham Ibn Al-`Abbas who was then his governor of Makkah. In the year 39 AH, the Imam sent `Ubaid Allah Ibn Al-`Abbas to oversee the Hajj season and lead the pilgrims in prayers as usual, but Mu`awiyah sent Yazid Ibn Shajarah Al-Ruhawi, ignoring what the Imam was doing. When `Ubaid Allah and Yazid met in Makkah, they disputed between themselves, and neither surrendered to the other! In the circumstances, it was agreed that Shaibah Ibn `Uthman Ibn Talhah, the custodian of the Ka`bah, should lead the pilgrims in prayers. The news of such developments must have caused a deep distress to the innocent Imam when it reached his ears!

The Out-Goers (Al-Khawarij or the Kharijites):

Then came the disturbing news about the mischiefs committed by Al-Khawarij, the *Kharijites*. They had killed Abd Allah, son of a distinguished Companion called Khabbab Ibn Al-Aratt, and had stabbed open the stomach of his pregnant wife. They also killed other innocent women. Nevertheless, they were meticulous in observing the religious rituals. They seemed to be the group of people referred to by the Prophet, peace and blessings be upon him, when one day someone came and told the Prophet:

"Be fair, O Muhammad!"
The Prophet told him:

"Woe to you. Who can be fair if I am not fair!"

`Umar Ibn Al-Khattab, who was then present, requested the Prophet's approval to kill him. The Prophet, peace and blessings be upon him, said:

"Leave him alone There are (or: There is going to be a group of) people who will be like him (as rough as he is). Yet they will be so meticulous in observing the worship rituals that one of you would look down at his own prayer compared to their prayer, and on his own fasting compared to theirs. Yet they deviate from the true religion in the same way as an arrow misses its target."

The Imam who was preparing to march on Syria had thus to change his course to meet those splitters or "Out-Goers." He met with their leaders and tried to reason with them, but his efforts were in vain. He addressed them:

"O band who has exited itself by futile argument and persistent denial (of the truth), deprived from knowing the truth by following your own desire for disputation. Your seductive souls have seduced you to break away from me and made you insist on that arbitration which you proposed and demanded against my wisdom, although I told you it was an insincere, dishonest stratagem. You opposed me obstinately and compelled me to follow your opinion. You are indeed of little intelligence and foolish-minded. Your leaders chose two men, and they pledged themselves before us to follow the terms of the Qur'an and not to deviate from its teachings. They went astray and disregarded the truth knowingly. Now tell us: how can you make shedding our blood lawful, running away from our unified stand, then you spread havoc, chasing innocent people and murdering them! That indeed is the real, evident loss!"

As a result of this address most of them dispersed. Of eighteen thousand, only four thousand dared to fight the Imam; and they were all finished, except nine of them who ran away in different directions. `Abd Allah Ibn Ibad was one of two who ran away to Oman. His followers survived till nowadays, although they might have modified their stand regarding the status of our great Imam.

Treacherous Murder of the Great Imam!:

This great genius, that noble soul, the undefeated and undefeatable warrior, Imam Ali Ibn Abi Talib who never employed a bodyguard, became an easy victim to a mean, awkward murderer, a Kharijite, who struck the Imam on the head with a poisoned sword when the Imam was about to enter Al-Kufah mosque for the dawn prayer on Friday, 17 Ramadan 40 AH.

An Intrigue to Slay the Three Major Political Figures:

Three members of the Kharijite group discussed among themselves the then current political crisis arising from the dispute over the question of the caliphate. They concluded that the best way to improve the situation was to kill the three major personalities involved in the dispute; namely, Imam Ali Ibn Abi Talib, Mu`awiyah Ibn Abi Sufyan, and `Amr Ibn Al-`As.

Mu`awiyah and `Amr ibn Al-`As Escape Death:

The task of killing Imam Ali was trusted to one of them called Abd Al-Rahman Ibn Muljam, and they agreed that the murder of the three personalities should be undertaken simultaneously so that the three would-be victims would be taken by surprise, not anticipating such an attack. Otherwise, if one or two of them were killed, the surviving one or two would take extra precautions and the plan might not work.

The would-be murderers went away, each to his destination. One, namely Abd Al-Rahman Ibn Muljam went to Al-Kufah, a town started by Caliph Umar Ibn Al-Khattab, like Al-Basrah, in order to be army resorts in view of their strategic positions. Imam Ali transferred his office to Al-Kufah for the same reason, and made it his capital. The other two murderers went away, one to Damascus, Syria, to kill Mu`awiyah, and the other went to Al-Fustat, Egypt, to kill `Amr Ibn Al-`As who had taken Egypt over after killing its governor appointed by the Imam, namely, Muhammad Ibn Abu Bakr, who was a stepson of the Imam from Fatimah Bint `Umais, a widow of Abu Bakr.

The date agreed to by the murderers was Friday, 17 Ramadan 40 AH, and the time was the dawn prayer, when each of the three would-be victims was to be on his way to the mosque.

`Amr Ibn Al-`As was lucky. He felt sick that morning and sent someone else, called Kharijah, to lead the congregation on his behalf. Poor Kharijah was killed, for the murderer thought that he was `Amr. Mu`awiyah was hit, but the stroke was not fatal. It cut a part of his bottom, and he was successfully treated. When his attacker was caught, he told him: "I am conveying to you a good tiding—Ibn Abi Talib has been killed." Mu`awiyah kept him in prison until the news came of the murder of the Imam. He cut his hand and foot and then set him free.

Only the Imam Becomes the Victim!:

Ibn Muljam went to Al-Kufah. He arrived there a few days before the day appointed for the crime. While he was staying in Al-Kufah, he fell in love with a beautiful girl called Qatami. He proposed to her to marry him, but she stipulated that her dower consisted of the payment to her of 3,000 dirhams, a slave girl, and a slave boy. In addition, and this was the most important part, he should slay Imam Ali. Her father and brother were killed on the day of Al-Nahrawan! Abd Al-Rahman argued with Qatami, "But if I should kill Ali and I am caught, I would be killed, and then I cannot have you." She replied: "If you kill him and escape safely, you would have done what you wanted to do and will have me as your wife. If you cannot escape and get killed, then that which you will have with Allah will be much greater and better for you." Abd Al-Rahman told Qatami: "I have agreed to your terms."

And so the criminal Abd Al-Rahman Ibn Muljam had more than one reason to motivate him to commit his serious crime! On the appointed day and at the agreed time, the criminal Abd Al-Rahman Ibn Muljam was hiding close to the entrance of the mosque in Al-Kufah. As usual, Imam Ali appeared on his way to the mosque early that morning, calling upon people to rise for the morning prayer, not accompanied by any bodyguard. It was therefore easy for the criminal to reach him. With his poisoned sword, the criminal hit him hard on the head, saying: "Ruling belongs to Allah, not to any one else." The Imam's head was broken and the sword reached his brain! The Imam fell on the ground. The criminal was captured. The Imam ordered people to go to perform their prayer and not to miss it. He himself prayed on his death mat. His nephew, Hudhaifah, son of the Imam's sister, Umm Hani', led the prayer in the mosque.

The Imam survived that Friday and Saturday and died on Sunday evening. He was laid to rest in Al-Kufah. May the Merciful Allah raise his status in Paradise and reward him abundantly for his eminent services.

It is a strange coincidence that the Imam was killed on the anniversary of one of the early glorious days, 17 Ramadan of the second Hijrah year, the day of Badr when he daringly came out from the Muslim camp to take up the challenge of `Utbah Ibn Rabi`ah, his brother Shaibah and his son Al-Walid. We may recall that the Imam finished Al-Walid, Hamzah killed `Utbah, and both he and Hamzah helped in finishing Shaibah!

In spite of the pain and the agony, the Imam, as remarked earlier, never lost his mental agility. He continued to let literary jewels flow from his chaste mouth. He then engaged his tongue in repeating the words la ilaha illa Allah (There is no deity but Allah), until he breathed his last on Sunday evening, 20 Ramadan 40 AH, aging sixty-three years!

While the Imam was struggling with death, the murderer was brought up before him, as he had been arrested by some of the Imam's devotees. The Imam recognized him and told him: "Do you remember such and such favors I had done to you?" The Imam then told his own men:

> "A soul for a soul. If I should die on account of his hitting me, slay him only and abuse not his body. I heard the Messenger of Allah, peace and blessings be upon him, forbid abusing a human body. If I should recover, I myself shall decide what to do to him, either forgive him or punish him. In the meantime, feed him well and torture him not. Provide him with a comfortable sleeping mat."

And addressing his sons, Al-Hasan and Al-Husain, the Imam said:

"O you sons of Abd Al-Muttalib! Do not shed Muslim blood profusely shouting the slogan: `The Commander of the Faithful has been slain.' Kill not because of me none but my murderer. If I die from his stroke, strike him once in retaliation. Mutilate not his body, because I heard the Messenger of Allah, peace and blessings be upon him, say: `Guard yourselves against mutilating the body of a living being, even if it be a mad dog.'"

The Imam's Bequest:

The Imam also dictated the following as his last injunction:

"This is the bequest that I am leaving behind. I, Ali Ibn Abi Talib, brother of Muhammad, peace and blessings be upon him, and his (paternal) cousin and companion. The first part of my bequest is that I bear witness that there is no deity but Allah and that Muhammad is His Messenger and His preferred choice. He (Allah) chose him according to His knowledge and made him the link with His creatures. Allah shall indeed raise the tombs' dwellers and shall bring people to account for their deeds. He verily knows that which lies in (people's) breasts.

"O my son Hasan! I enjoin upon you the same recommendation the Messenger of Allah had given me: Stick to your house, recall your sins till it makes you weep, and let not (success in) this near world your main objective. My son, keep up your prayers regularly at their appointed times and pay the zakat (alms) to its legitimate recipients when it is due. Maintain silence when you are in doubt. Be moderate and fair whether you are in a relaxed or in a tight mood. Be a thoughtful neighbor and a generous host, and be sympathetic to the weak and to those who suffer misfortune. Do good to your kindred and be helpful to the poor. Show them respect and keep not away from them. One of the most meritorious kinds of worship is to be humble with the lower strata of society. Remember always death and let not materialism get hold of you. You are always exposed to death and an easy target of misfortune. Fear always Almighty Allah privately and publicly. Comply with the demands of the *Shari`ah* (law) and never deviate from it in word or in action. Delay not the demands of the day of the Hereafter, and fulfill from the worldly demands that which is righteous. Keep away from suspicious situations, and associate not with suspicious elements. Association with such fellows is corruptive."

"Struggle to earn Allah's pleasure. Forbid obscenity and evils and command all that is good. Be friendly for Allah's sake. Love the righteous for the sake of his piety. Keep aloof from the sinful person without offending him, hating him in your heart, revealing your resentment of his deeds through your good deeds. Sit not in the way of the traffic, be not argumentative and go not along with a silly person. Be reasonable in domestic living and exaggerate not in worship. Do of it the degree you can constantly maintain with no hardship. Your safety lies in your silence. Store for the future, you will gain; and learn where goodness lies. Keep Allah always in your mind. Be sympathetic to the youngsters and respectful of the old. When you get food, give some of it in charity before you consume your share. Fast as many days as you can, for fasting is the bodily contribution and is physically healthy. Struggle against your desire, be on your guard when you have a companion, and keep away from your enemy. Join the gatherings of remembrance of Allah and pray often to Allah. Be good to your (half) brother Muhammad, you know how much I love him. As for Al-Husain, he is your full brother, the son of your mother and your father. I trust you all to Allah, and I plead to Him alone that He may make good your fortune and may He protect you from people of violence. Patience, patience until Allah decides and settles this matter. There is neither might nor strength but with Allah, the Most High, the Great!"

Thereafter the Imam uttered no words, except that he was heard repeating the *shahadah* till his last breath. May Almighty Allah, the Merciful, the Compassionate, bless the righteous soul of the Imam and ennoble his face!

The Imam's washing was attended to by his sons Al-Hasan, Al-Husain, Muhammad, and their cousin Abd Allah Ibn Ja`far. He was shrouded in three simple white wrappers, and was laid to rest in Al-Najaf, in southern Iraq. The funeral prayer service over his noble body was led by his son, Al-Hasan.

It seems that the Imam had some sort of premonition and somehow felt that he was approaching the end of his earthly life. During that month, Ramadan, on the 17th of which he was killed, he used to have his breakfast meal one day with his son Al-Hasan, one day with Al-Husain, and one day with Abd Allah Ibn Ja`far. Each time he only had three or four morsels (bites). When he was urged to eat more, he responded:

> "To meet Allah with an empty stomach will be better for me. It is only a matter of a few days before I meet with my Lord!"

....

O Imam Ali Ibn Abi Talib! May Almighty Allah be pleased with you and may He let your face always shine with honor and nobility. Millions of people in all generations admire you, love you, and wish that they could lay their lives as ransom for yours, willing to die and give their own lives so that you could succeed in your struggle for justice, for the elevation of the ummah, and for the betterment of the conditions of the poor and the week. You never prostrated before an idol. While you were still a little boy you accompanied Sayyidina Muhammad, who was destined to be the last messenger of Allah, to the Ka`bah under the night cover, climbed over Muhammad's shoulders, and pushed the solemn idols to the ground, to let the polytheists reflect, if they had sound mind, over the futility of worshipping figures that could not defend themselves! You used to go with the Prophet for prayers in the valleys outside Makkah, away from the malicious eyes of the polytheists.

The world of Islam owes you a great deal of debt for willingly agreeing to protect the Prophet's life by sleeping on his sleeping mat and covering yourself with his own mantle to confound the murderous youthful party waiting in ambush at the step of the door of the Prophet's house, thus giving the Prophet enough time to leave the town un-noticed and reach a hiding place before the enemies could be alerted to the Prophet's disappearance and start a thorough search for him in all directions. You were the first member of the small Muslim army to dare and respond to the polytheists' fearful challenges for duel fighting, and each challenger lost his life at your hand—but only after inviting each one of them to embrace Islam or at least to assume a neutral attitude. Their persistent menacing attitude led to their end with your sword.

You were the first to stand firm by the Prophet at the critical moments on the days of Uhud and Hunain, in spite of the wounds you yourself had sustained. You led the vanguards on the day of the conquest of Makkah, and you were the one who could venture to split open the powerful fortresses of Khaibar.

No words can be sufficient to convey your special merits, your legendary courage, your gallantry, your generosity, your clemency, your magnanimity, your asceticism, or your piety or your shrewdness, which was tempered by your honesty, your sincerity, and your fear of Allah. It is only regretted that your caliphate started during the time of an exceptional crisis, which led to troublesome misunderstanding and diverted you from contributing more constructively to the elevation of the *ummah* during your reign! Allah knows best, and He alone can reward you!

Echo of the Imam's Death:

When the news about the Imam's death spread, a wave of deep sorrow and sympathy swept all over the Muslim world. Companions who had hesitated to support the Imam and preferred neutrality, like Abd Allah Ibn Umar, regretted having left the Imam alone to fend for himself in what is described by a modern author as a jungle of wolves!

Even Mu`awiyah himself is said to have been struck with deep grief. It is related that when his wife saw him weeping, she said to him:

"How come! You fought him hard when he was alive, and you now cry when he dies?"

Mu`awiyah told her:

"You do not know how much (useful) knowledge of jurisprudence and of other areas is going to be buried with him!"

In spite of the bitter dispute between them, Mu`awiyah used to send a request to the Imam for an answer through an intermediary, when he was confronted with a difficult problem. For example, Imam Malik in his renowned work *Al-Muwatta'*, relates that Mu`awiyah sent a message to the Imam through Abu Musa Al-Ash`ari regarding a problem he encountered. The Imam gave Abu Musa the answer. The problem, it seems, was concerned with the inheritance of a hermaphrodite person, as related by some other authorities.

Mu`awiyah became the undisputed caliph after the Imam's death and the surrender by Imam Al-Hasan, the Imam's son, of his claim to the caliphate. When he was called upon by some of Imam Ali's former supporters, he used to ask them why they were so solidly for Ali and opposed to him. Mu`awiyah, who was reputed to be a clement person, listened attentively and displayed no traces of anger. Let us quote one or two examples.

Mu`awiyah once asked someone of the Imam's supporters called Dirar Ibn Dumrah, saying:

"Describe Ali to me."

"Please forgive me," Dirar pleaded to Mu`awiyah.

"I swear you must describe Ali for me," Mu`awiyah insisted.

"If I have to do so," said Dirar, "I should say: By Allah, Ali was a far-sighted man, stoutly strong, decisive when he spoke, fair and just in his judgment. His knowledge was so great that it almost was bursting on all sides. His tongue always uttered words of wisdom. He cared least about this material world and its seductive factors. He felt better by himself at the night time, when his eyes often shed tears profusely over long reflection. He was contended with rough material for clothes, and with little poor food stuff. Among us, he behaved just like one of us. He politely answered our enquiries and graciously obliged when we invited him. Yet, by Allah, in spite of his modesty and his being so close to us, we awed him a great deal. He respected especially religious people and kept close to the poor. The strong among us could not expect from him special favors on account of his strength, nor did the weak despair of his justice.

"Allah is my witness, I saw him once (from a distance) retired by himself when night had let down its curtains and its stars had sunk deeply, and I overheard him saying, wile holding his beard and writhing like a snake, and crying like a bereaved person: `O *Dunia* (the material world), leave me alone. Go away and try to deceive someone else. Why do you cross my way and struggle to seduce me? No, no. I have divorced you in an irrecoverable divorce. Your age is short, your danger is grave and your joy is polluted! Oh, the provision is insufficient and the journey is long and the road is dangerous."

Tears were seen running from the eyes of Mu`awiyah, who then said;

"He was truly so. May Allah bestow His mercy upon Al-Hasan's father. O Dirar! How do you feel about his loss?"

"The same degree of grief suffered by a mother whose son was slain in her lap. So her tears never dry up, nor will her distress wane!," Dirar answered.

A lady called Sawdah Binti `Imarah from the tribe of Hamadan, called once on Mu`awiyah after the death of the Imam to complain to him about the behavior of his governor of the district in which she lived. Once he saw her, Mu`awiyah began to scorn her for her support of the Imam and for instigating people against Mu`awiyah, especially during the battle at *Siffin*. He then asked her, "What do you want?" She said, "Verily Almighty Allah shall bring you to account concerning our life and concerning that which Allah has made you in charge of our matters. You have been sending us people to rule over us and oppress us in your name, destroying us as if he were harvesting ears of corn, and treading over us as if he were treading over rye! He humiliates us, and lets us taste bitter death. That (Governor) Bishr Ibn Artah, since he descended upon us, has been slaying our men, wrongfully taking away our wealth although we are a people of power and fortitude. We could take the law in our own hand, but we prefer to be law-abiding citizens. We shall be grateful if you should remove him. Otherwise we can only take our case to Allah!

Mu`awiyah responded:

"How dare you speak to me as such, as if you are threatening me! I may just send you back to him on the back of a rough beast and leave it to him to deal with you."

Sawdah lowered her head a little, and then sang a poem:

"May the Lord bless a body resting in
a grave in which justice has teen buried!
He made a covenant with truth, with justice,
never desirous any alternative,
And he and justice became a twain!"

Mu`awiyah asked: Who is it that you mean, Sawdah?"

"By Almighty Allah, he is the Commander of the Faithful, Ali Ibn Abi Talib, may Allah be pleased with him. I once called upon him regarding a man he had appointed to take care of our payments, but he overstepped his limits. When I went to see him (Imam Ali), he was about to start his prayers. When he glanced at me, he turned towards me with a friendly face, sympathetic and kind, and asked: `Do you need anything?' I said: `Yes,' and submitted to him my case. He cried, turned to the qiblah, and said: `O Allah! You are my Witness. I have not ordered them to wrong your creatures or neglect their obligations towards You.' He then brought out from his pocket a piece of skin and wrote a message to that agent saying:

"In the name of Allah, the Merciful, the Compassionate. Now has come unto you a clear sign from your Lord! So, give just measure and weight, and withhold not from the people the things that are their due, and do no mischief on the earth after it has been set in order. That will be best for you if you are true believers. When you have read this letter from me, keep it until someone comes to take it from you. Peace be upon you."

She added that the Imam handed over that letter to her to give it to that governor who was thereby relieved from his post."

Mu`awiyah ordered that she be given what she needed. It is related that Mu`awiyah then asked her: "Would Ali have given you all this?" And she replied: "No, by Allah. Not even a single hair of a camel, from the properties of Muslims."

The Imam's Children:

The Imam begot fifteen sons; namely:

- Al-Hasan,
- Al-Husain,
- Muhsin, (who died young). Their mother was Al-Sayyidah Fatimah, the Prophet's daughter, who also begot him two daughters: Ummu Kulthum Senior (Al-Kubra) and Zainab Senior (Al-Kubra). Al-Sayyidah Fatimah died about six months after the Prophet, peace and blessings

be upon him. The Imam did not remarry until after her death. Al-Sayyidah Fatimah is described as Al-Batul (the one who has no match, or the one devoted to piety and worship). The Prophet, peace and blessings be upon him, asked Fatimah Bint Asad, the Imam's mother, to undertake the external needs of the household of Imam Ali, whereas his daughter Fatimah undertook the internal services.

- Muhammad Al-Akbar (Muhammad Senior), whose mother was Khawlah Binti Ja`far Ibn Qais of the Hanifah tribe. So he is called Muhammad Ibn Al-Hanafiyyah.
- Abd Allah,
- Abu Bakr. The mother of these last two sons was Laila Binti Mas`ud Al-Nahshali.
- Al-`Abbas Al-`Akbar (Al-Abbas Senior),
- Uthman,
- Ja`far,
- Abd Allah (The mother of these four sons was Ummu Al-Banin Binti Hizam Al-Wahidiyyah).
- Muhammad Al-Asghar (Muhammad Junior), from a slave mother.
- Yahya, and
- Awn. (Their mother was Asma' Binti `Umais, a widow of Abu Bakr and mother of his son, Muhammad, who became a stepson of the Imam and was appointed by him governor of Egypt, replacing Qais Ibn Sa`d, a shrewd man who was feared by Mu`awiyah, who spread an untrue rumor that Qais was getting on his side, causing the Imam to relieve him, replacing him at first by Al-Ashtar, who was given a poisoned drink while he was on the way to Egypt. In the series of attacks by the forces of Mu`awiyah on the territories under Imam Ali, following the tahkim fiasco, Mu`awiyah's forces, led by `Amr Ibn Al-`As, defeated Muhammad Ibn Abu Bakr. It is said that his body was put inside the stomach of a dead donkey! When the news reached the ears of the Imam, he was deeply grieved and said, "They have been relieved of an enemy and we have lost a good friend!"
- `Umar Al-Akbar, and

- Muhammad Al-Awsat (Muhammad, the Middle one). He is the son of Umamah, daughter of Zainab, the Prophet's daughter, and Abu Al-`As Ibn Al-Rabi`. This Umamah is the Prophet's granddaughter who used, when she was very young, to play with the Prophet, peace and blessings be upon him, and jump over him when he was prostrating, and the Prophet remained in that position till she moved away by herself! The Imam married her on the recommendation of her aunt, Al-Sayyidah Fatimah.

The Imam begot the following daughters:

- Ummu Kulthum (who was married to Umar Ibn Al-Khattab),
- Ruqayyah (full sister of Umar Senior),
- Zainab Senior (full sister of Al-Hasan and Al-Husain),
- Ummu al-Husn,
- Ramlah Senior,
- Zainab Junior,
- Ummu Kulthum Junior,
- Ummu Hani',
- Maimunah,
- Ramlah Junior,
- Zainab Junior,
- Ummu Kulthum Junior,
- Fatimah,
- Umamah,
- Khadijah,
- Ummu al-Khair,
- Ummu Salamah,
- Ummu Ja`far,
- Jumanah, and
- Taqiyyah.

The Imam's Intense Intelligence:

Imam Ali was endowed with a quick, sharp, incisive, mathematical mind. We may relate here some interesting stories in which the Imam's sharp intelligence revealed itself.

The Imam was once interrupted while he was delivering a sermon from the pulpit by someone who asked him how to distribute the inheritance of someone who had died leaving a wife, his parents and two daughters. The Imam instantly answered:

"The wife's share becomes one ninth."

This answer is in fact the result of a long analysis with a number of steps. Ordinarily, we have to decide on the original share of each of these heirs, in the following way:

- The wife takes one eighth, in view of the presence of an inheriting child.

- The deceased's father and mother take one sixth each.

- The two daughters take two thirds of the inheritance.

So the total will be: $1/8 + 1/6 + 1/6 + 2/3 = 3/24 + 4/24 + 4/24 + 16/24 = 27/24$. This means that the share becomes less than 1/24 in view of the increase of the total of the shares which are so fixed and prescribed. So the one eighth, the original share due to the wife out of twenty-four total shares, has become three shares out of a total of twenty-seven, which is one ninth. The Imam's mind went through this complex mathematical process in a second!

Another case in which the Imam's intelligence revealed itself is the case of a woman who complained to him:

"How come that I receive from my deceased brother's estate only one *dinar* out of a six hundred *dinars* estate?"

The Imam said:

"Did your brother leave, besides you, a wife, his mother, and two or more daughters and twelve brothers?"

"Yes," the woman replied.

"Then your share is one *dinar* only."

The Imam, may Allah be pleased with his soul, gave the answer instantly, but the analysis is as follows: The wife's share is 1/8. The daughters' share is 2/3, and the mother's is 1/6. The remainder is to be given to twelve brothers and their sister, as the male takes twice as much as the female. So in terms of actual money, the mother gets 100 *dinars*, the wife takes 75 *dinars*, the two daughters take 400 *dinars*, which makes a total of 575 *dinars* taken by heirs whose shares are fixed by the Holy Qur'an. This leaves a balance of 25 *dinars* for the twelve brothers, each of whom takes two *dinars*, and the sister takes one.

This very complex calculation was made instantly and analyzed by the Imam's rare mind in a split second with no pen or paper!

The Imam's Ability to Respond with Persuasive Answers:

Once the Imam was asked: "How could Allah (God) bring all people to account (on the Day of Judgment) while they are so many?"

The Imam answered:

"As much He has been able to provide for them all in spite of their huge number."

The Imam's Mathematical Brilliance:

This has been demonstrated already in a number of stories related earlier. However, let's add the following story. Two men came up to the Imam to settle their dispute. Let's call them A and B. They had had a meal together to which A contributed 5 loaves and B contributed 3 loaves. The problem was that a third person, C, shared the meal with them and paid them 8 *dirhams* and went away. When A and B wanted to divide the eight *dirhams* between them, they quarrelled. A said: "I should get 5 *dirhams* and you, B, get only three dirhams. This is a fair distribution," he added, "as it agrees with the rate of the loaves each of us had contributed." B refused and insisted on an equal division of the *dirhams*, each getting four *dirhams*.

As they could not agree, A and B went up to the Imam to settle their dispute. The Imam told B: "Your friend has been more than fair to you. He contributed fifteen thirds of a loaf whereas you contributed nine thirds. Since you are supposed to have eaten an equal amount each (eight thirds out of a total of twenty four), C consumed only one eighth of your contribution (which means that B was only entitled to one *dirham*.)

The Imam's brilliance as a careful and precise judge can be revealed in the story of four young men who drank till the point of intoxication. Then they quarrelled and fought each other with knives. Two of them were killed. The relatives of the two victims applied to Caliph Ali for the blood wealth (compensation). The family of each victim claimed a full *diyah* (blood compensation). The Imam passed a judgment according to which the family of each victim got only one quarter of a *diyah* in view of the fact that the two victims had to share in the responsibility for drinking to the point of intoxication and carrying dangerous weapons. In fact, it was possible that they had killed each other, the Imam remarked.

It was, in fact, the Imam's deep commitment to the principle of justice that, when he was elected caliph, he withdrew rich gifts given by his predecessor from the treasury (*Bait Al-Mal*), including one hundred thousand *dirhams* given to the caliph's son-in-law, (husband of his daughter A'ishah), and two hundred thousand given to Abu Sufyan Ibn Harb, father of Mu`awiyah!

In this context, we may mention in passing that this A'ishah, Caliph Uthman's daughter, screamed recalling her father's murder in front of Mu`awiyah when he came to visit Al-Madinah as the undisputed ruler of the world of Islam. (Imam Ali had died and his son, Imam Al-Hasan, surrendered the claim of the caliphate to Mu`awiyah in order to preserve Muslim blood). A'ishah intended to provoke Mu`awiyah to take revenge for her father. Mu`awiyah, who fought hard the Imam on the pretext of demanding revenge for Uthman's blood, calmed her down and excused himself of undertaking that task to preserve Muslim unity!

Let's now conclude the noble biography of the Imam by relating a moving story that denotes the Imam's deep sense of justice and humility.

The Imam's shield, which was included in a camel's load going to Siffin, dropped. It was picked up by a person from amongst the People of the Book. The Imam saw the shield later in the hand of that person in Al-Kufah and recognized it. As it had been given to him as a gift by the Prophet, peace and blessings be upon him, the Imam asked that person to give him back his shield. He refused, not knowing that he was the caliph. So both the Imam and that person went to the court and both stood before the judge, (Al-Qadi Shuraih, who had been appointed in that post by the Imam).

Imam Ali brought two witnesses, including his son Al-Husain. The Qadi said: "O Commander of the Faithful. As you know a son cannot be a witness in favor of his father, and since you have no more than one legitimate witness, I cannot pass a judgment in this case in your favor."

Imam Ali, with no malice or anger, surrendered to that judgment, and that non-Muslim person went away with the shield! However, soon that non-Muslim person reflected on his own and, admiring the Islamic justice and the modesty of the caliph, returned to proclaim the truth, to hand over the shield back to the Imam, and to declare his conversion to Islam.

Chapter IX

Selections from the Jewel-Like Words of the Imam

Imam Ali is described by the Prophet as the Gate to Knowledge. The Imam was also acknowledged to be the most eloquent person after the Prophet. His sentences are often short, sometimes easily rhymed and of penetrating meaning. Let us quote here some of them:

- The more wisdom, the lesser the speech.
- An advice given publicly is an insult.
- It is a blessing that a person realizes his own limitations.
- A person is an enemy to whatever he does not know.
- Envy only leads to distress.
- The worse enemy is he who conceals his strategy.
- Taking revenge is not a victory.
- The mind lies behind the tongue.
- People are sleepy; they wake up when they die!
- Worrying and good health cannot go together.
- Peoples of integrity appreciate other people's favors.
- A person's value depends on his achievement.
- Whoever aspires to see his Lord (God), let him first attempt to see his own soul!
- A sweet tongue earns many friends.
- Those who are mean save their wealth for a disaster or an heir.
- Doing wrongs to others is no victory.
- Anxiety over a disaster means more suffering.
- Failure to consult (over important issues) leads to making errors.
- Plenty is nobility.
- Ignorance is the worst sickness.
- Your tongue goes along with your training.
- Repetition of an apology is a reminder of the injury.
- Hypocrisy is humiliation.

- Undeserved fortune is like an orchard over a heap of trash.
- Seek not that which is not your likeness.
- Lending an ear to backbiting is participation in the evil transgression.
- Greed leads to humiliation.
- Be not a slave to your desire, lest you become worse than a slave person.
- Enmity is painful to the heart.
- Flattering is hypocrisy.
- Grab an opportunity before it becomes too late.
- Nobility lies in good manners.
- Wisdom is the greatest asset.
- Expose not yourself lest you get destroyed.
- The heart of an insolent person is in his mouth, and the tongue of a wise fellow is in his heart.
- If you have a chance over your enemy, be gratefully magnanimous.
- Slips of the tongue reveal the secrets of the mind.
- Let wisdom control your tongue; let not your tongue be ahead of your heart.
- Knowledge raises, ignorance lowers.
- Knowledge is better than wealth. Knowledge protects you, whereas wealth needs your protection. Knowledge rules, and wealth is ruled.
- The envious hurts the innocent.
- A person may run after his own misfortune.
- Despair (of what is in the others's hands) is liberty, anticipation is humiliation.
- Hatred blinds the heart.
- A wise person learns from the others' experiences.
- Meanness is the source of shortcomings.
- Uncritical endorsement is hypocrisy.
- Habitual disputation is disruptive.
- Transgression is self-destruction.
- Obliging cuts the foul tongue.
- Honor goes along with wisdom, and manners follow one's own roots.
- Look for good manners before asking about a persn's roots.
- Stupidity is the worst poverty.
- Self-conceit is the worst property.
- Wisdom is the greatest fortune.
- Greed is humiliating.
- A soft stem has many branches.
- The heart of the impertinent is in his mouth, and the tongue of the wise is in his heart.
- I am bothered by two things: a careless man of knowledge

and an ignorant saintly person. One offends the people by his violence, and the other leads them astray.

- A parent has a right over his (her) child, and the child has a right over its parent. The child must obey its parent's demands, unless a parent makes an unlawful demand, and the parent has to give his (her) child a good name, has to bring it up well and to teach the child the Holy Qur'an.

- Hurt not women, for they deserve our sympathy. We are commanded to avoid hurting even unbelieving women. (We are to be unlike) the pre-Islamic men who used to abuse women by beating them with a stick and throwing stones at them, a shameful practice which brought dishonor to those who indulged in it and to their offspring.

- By Allah, Mu`awiyah is not more shrewd than I. But he does not hesitate to deceive and deviate (from the proper course). Had it not been for my hatred of deception, I could have been the most cunning person.

- A person is a mind and a form. A dull mind deprives him of his soul.

- The key to Paradise is forbearance, and the key to honor is humility.

- No asset is greater than contentedness.

- The best speech is a short meaningful word.

- In forgiving lies your comfort.

- Mix with noble people, you become one of them; and keep away from evil people to protect yourself from their evils.

- Telling the truth delivers, telling a lie is failure.

- Many a stranger may be more helpful than a kin.

- The best part of your wealth is that which meets your basic needs.

- Those who live in ease fail to appreciate the plight of those in need.

- Be on your guard with him to whom you trusted your secrets.

- Self-respect restrains one's desire.

- Life keeps changing: a day for you and a day against you.

- Trusting before experimenting is weakness.

- Contentedness is the decoration of the poor.

- People are the children of this near (material) world. Therefore, blame them not for loving their mother.

- When Allah bestows His favors upon a person, He makes people be in need for him.

-This *dunia* (the material world) is rotten.Whoever runs after it, it lets him forbear mixing with dogs.

- This *dunia* and the Hereafter are as far apart as the East and the West. When a person approaches either of them, the other gets further away.

- No trade is profitable as much as righteousness, and there is no profit that can compare with Allah's pleasure.
- Be not overjoyed with worldly success, and be not distressed over that which you may miss from it. Be more concerned with that which can benefit you after death.
- Man is a growing, sensitive body.
- Store from this transitory life for the eternal Hereafter, from this *dunia* for your death, from your good health to your illness, and from the time of ease to the time of poverty.
- Now you live at your home, tomorrow you will rest in your tomb!
- The best virtues of women are the worst vices of men: pride, cowardice, and meanness; (pride protects a woman's honor, cowardice keeps her away from indecencies, and meanness protects her husband's properties and hers from extravagance).
- A wise, restrained enemy is better than a careless friend.
- Avoidance of sins is safer than repentance with remorse.
- Reform yourself before lecturing to others.
- Time changes. Sometimes it is on your side, and sometimes it turns against you. When it is in your favor, be on your guard; when it turns against you, despair not.
- This near world is like a cadaver. Those who seek it have to tolerate the company of the dogs.
- Seek knowledge and be prepared with its tools: intelligence, eagerness, patience, means, guidance, and time.
- Store from this transitory world to the eternal life. Take from your life for your death, from your health for your illness, and from your wealth for your need. Remember: now you are at home. but tomorrow you will dwell in the grave!
- Verily Almighty Allah has assigned a share for the poor in the wealth of the rich. The reason for the hunger of the poor is the extravagance of the rich.
- I cannot be happy with being called "Commander of the Faithful" unless I share the hardships sustained by the people. By Almighty Allah, if I wish, I would have the best kinds of food on my table each meal and would have my clothes made of the finest material. But I will not give in to my desire and shall never go to bed with a full stomach while those around go to bed with empty stomachs.

والحمد لله أولاً وآخراً

الإمام الغالب
علي بن أبي طالب